FLORENCE

where to find

GIOTTO · BRUNELLESCHI
MASACCIO · DONATELLO
THE DELLA ROBBIA FAMILY
FRA ANGELICO
BOTTICELLI · GHIRLANDAIO
MICHELANGELO

Alta Macadam

SCALA

Acknowledgements

The author is indebted to numerous friends for their assistance during the preparation of this book, but she would like to thank in particular Laura Ridi at Scala for her sensitive and careful editorial work. Marilena Vecchi, of Scala, also provided much professional help at proof stage.
Laura Corti and Piero Colacicchi made some helpful suggestions about art historical details in the guide, and Mark Roberts generously supplied the English translations of the Italian texts quoted.

Photographic acknowledgements: SCALA Picture Library (M. Falsini, S. Lampredi) except for p. 173 below (Fototeca Casa Buonarroti)

Printed in Italy by "Arti Grafiche" StampArte Calenzano (Florence), 2007

Page 3: Baldassarre Lanci, *View of Florence*, detail.
Florence, Gabinetto dei Disegni e delle Stampe degli Uffizi

THE DELLA ROBBIA FAMILY
70

FRA ANGELICO
98

SANDRO BOTTICELLI
108

DOMENICO GHIRLANDAIO
128

MICHELANGELO BUONARROTI
146

GIOTTO

G iotto di Bondone (1266/7-1337) was born in the Mugello valley some 40 kilometres north of Florence at Vespignano just outside the little country town of Vicchio. He introduced a new style of painting which was to have a profound influence on the course of Italian art. His

Benedetto da Maiano, *Portrait of Giotto*. Florence, Duomo

painting has a realism, monumentality, and sense of volume which had never been achieved in medieval painting or by his master Cimabue. His figures are given an intensely human significance, and it was Bernard Berenson who first talked of the concept of 'tactile values' in his works.

He was immediately recognized by his contemporaries as a great painter. He was admired in his lifetime by Petrarch and Boccaccio, and his friend Dante mentioned him in his *Divina Commedia* (*Purgatorio*; Canto XI, 94-96):

Credette Cimabue nella pintura
Tener lo campo e ora ha Giotto il grido
Sì che la fama di colui è scura…
[Cimabue thought he held the field
In painting and now Giotto is the cry
The other's fame obscured]

He was commemorated in 1490 in the Duomo, his burial place, with an idealized bust by Benedetto da Maiano in a medallion and an inscription by Poliziano. In later centuries his works

were closely studied by numerous artists including Masaccio, Michelangelo, and Leonardo da Vinci.

Among his famous masterpieces outside Florence is the fresco cycle in the lovely Scrovegni chapel in Padua, painted at the height of his power (1303-05), the only one by him which survives intact. It depicts the story of Christian redemption through the lives of Mary and Christ, and the superb colouring, another characteristic of Giotto's works, is here extremely well preserved. Giotto is thought also to have designed the chapel itself.

Although it was in the upper and lower churches of San Francesco in Assisi that Giotto achieved his greatest fame, documentary evidence is lacking about his work here. The well-known frescoes of the St Francis cycle in the upper church are generally dated to the last decade of the 13th century, and although traditionally thought to be early works by Giotto and assistants (and mentioned as such by Vasari) they are not nowadays attributed to him by all scholars who also still discuss into which period of his activity they fall. Giotto is also thought to have been involved in the two remarkable Old Testament scenes illustrating the story of Isaac in the upper register of the south wall of the upper church. It seems that he worked in the lower church some twenty years later (although also here there are various attribution problems and differing theories about dates). It is known that Giotto received commissions for a number of other Franciscan fresco cycles besides those in Assisi and Florence, including two in Rimini and Padua, both now lost. He also worked for the papacy in Rome (and probably in Avignon), the Anjou in Naples and the Visconti in Milan.

Very few of his works are signed and he must have had a large workshop so that art historians still discuss the attribution of many of his works, and the extent of the intervention of his workshop. He had nine sons, two of whom worked with him as painters, but the identification of the most skilled of his assistants is still a subject of study. His frescoes in Santa Croce in Florence had a fundamental influence on Florentine painting and the Giottesque school continued to flourish in the city throughout the 14th century when Florence suffered severely from the Black Death which effectively stifled other innovative artistic movements during that century. Some of Giotto's greatest followers, whose frescoes can also be seen in Santa Croce, include Maso di Banco, Giovanni da Milano, and Taddeo Gaddi.

CAMPANILE

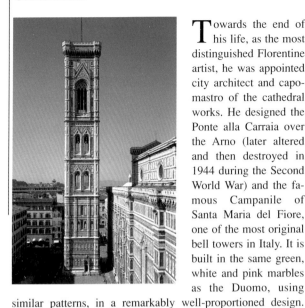

Towards the end of his life, as the most distinguished Florentine artist, he was appointed city architect and capo-mastro of the cathedral works. He designed the Ponte alla Carraia over the Arno (later altered and then destroyed in 1944 during the Second World War) and the famous Campanile of Santa Maria del Fiore, one of the most original bell towers in Italy. It is built in the same green, white and pink marbles as the Duomo, using similar patterns, in a remarkably well-proportioned design. Giotto began its construction in 1334, but it was completed by Andrea Pisano and Francesco Talenti in 1343-59. The lowest row of bas-reliefs by Andrea Pisano (the originals are now in the Museo dell'Opera del Duomo) may also have been designed by Giotto.

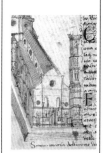

Marco Rustici, drawing from a 15th century codex of the Duomo and Campanile. Florence, Library of the Seminario Maggiore

SANTA CROCE

The Cappella Peruzzi and the Cappella Bardi in Santa Croce have important painted decoration by Giotto commissioned by two of the richest and most powerful merchant families in the city. In the 18th century, when the works of Giotto were not appreciated, they were covered with plaster and the lower scenes were destroyed to make way for the sepulchral monuments and altars which were erected against the walls. They were only rediscovered in 1841-52 when they were re-

stored by Gaetano Bianchi and others who carefully repainted the missing parts. But in a subsequent restoration in 1957-61 the repainting was removed since at that time Bianchi's solution was considered unethical by some restorers (although some of Bianchi's works for the two chapels are still preserved in a room off the sacristy).

Unfortunately both chapels are now difficult to examine in detail since they are cordoned off at the entrances, and the coin-operated lights illuminate the walls for only a short period.

St Francis receiving the Stigmata

St Francis stripping off his Garments

The Funeral of St Francis (top right); *The Ordeal by Fire before the Sultan of Egypt* (below)

Cappella Bardi

The fresco cycle in the Cappella Bardi, with *Scenes from the Life of St Francis*, was certainly designed by Giotto but it is possible that some of the frescoes were executed by his pupils. Their date is still discussed by scholars, but they are usually thought to have been executed in his maturity around 1320 or even 1330. They were designed to be seen from the centre of the chapel. On the entrance arch is the *Saint receiving the Stigmata*, and on the vault, *Poverty, Chastity, Obedience*, and the *Triumph of St Francis*. On the end wall are Franciscan saints, including *St Clare* (with a particularly beautiful head) and the three scenes on the left wall show the beardless *Saint stripping off his Garments, Appearing to St Anthony at Arles*, and the *Death of St Francis*. On the right wall the *Saint is receiving the Rule of the Order, is being tried by fire before the Sultan*, and *Appearing to Brother Augustine and Bishop Guido of Assisi*. The delightful altarpiece showing *St Francis and Scenes from his Life* is a Florentine work of the late 13th century.

MUSEO DELL'OPERA DI SANTA CROCE

Fragments of stained glass

Three fragments from a large stained glass window at the end of the south aisle of Santa Croce have recently been identified as works on a design by Giotto. They depict a prophet in a tondo and two martyred saints in lunettes.

Cappella Peruzzi

The mural paintings in the Cappella Peruzzi, not true frescoes, were carried out by Giotto around 1310 or 1320. Unfortunately they, too, are damaged and in extremely poor condition. They were designed to be seen from the entrance to the chapel. In the archivolt are eight heads of *Prophets* and in the

Zacharias and the Angel

Ascent of St John the Evangelist into Heaven

The Raising of Drusiana (left)

vault, the symbols of the *Evangelists*. On the right wall are *Scenes from the Life of St John the Evangelist* (his *Vision at Patmos*, *The Raising of Drusiana*, and his *Ascent into Heaven*) and on the left wall *Scenes from the Life of St John the Baptist* (*Zacharias and the Angel*, *the Birth of St John*, and *Herod's Feast*). The architectural settings contain numerous references to classical antiquity.

Cappella Baroncelli

Coronation of the Virgin, and detail from the central scene

The painting of the *Coronation of the Virgin* in the Cappella Baroncelli is one of four polyptychs by Giotto painted for this church, probably with the help of his workshop. It is signed by the master, and is one of the few works by Giotto which has remained in the chapel for which it was painted. The iconography is unusual since the single scene of the Coronation of the Virgin is divided into five panels, against a rich gold ground. It is today possible to examine the painting from close up and it is well illuminated. This chapel, in the south transept, has very fine frescoes by Taddeo Gaddi who worked with Giotto for many years and was his most faithful pupil.

Detail from the fresco with *Paradise* showing the portrait of the young Dante

MUSEO NAZIONALE DEL BARGELLO

Cappella della Maddalena

Other frescoes almost certainly in part by Giotto are those in the Cappella della Maddalena (or del Podestà) in the Palazzo del Bargello (now part of the Bargello Museum). When these were discovered in the 19th century (at the same time as those in Santa Croce) they were acclaimed as autograph works by Giotto. They contain an inscription with the date 1337, the year of Giotto's death, so that it is now thought that he probably only began some of the scenes but that they were finished after his death. They represent *Hell* (on the entrance wall, only fragments of which survive) and *Paradise* (or the *Last Judgement*) on the short wall opposite, and *Stories from the Life of St Mary Magdalen* and *Life of St John the Baptist* on the other two walls. They are unfortunately very poorly preserved and large areas have been lost altogether, although they are well lit and now much easier to view than the frescoed chapels by Giotto in Santa Croce. It is thought that Giotto himself is most likely to have worked on the scene of *Paradise*, which includes a well-known portrait of Dante as a young man dressed in a maroon hat and cloak behind the kneeling figure on the right.

GALLERIA DEGLI UFFIZI

Badia Polyptych

This painting of the *Madonna and Child with four Saints* is displayed in the same room as Giotto's *Maestà*. Lorenzo Ghiberti in his *Commentari* (circa 1450) records that he saw an altarpiece by Giotto in the Badia Fiorentina, but this painting was not identified as that work until the 20th century when its provenance was confirmed. It is an early work (1300) and considerably damaged. The carpentry of the lovely frame is also interesting.

Madonna and Child Enthroned (*Maestà*)

T he most important painting by Giotto still in Florence is the huge *Maestà* displayed in the first room of paintings of the gallery as a clear demonstration of Giotto's fundamental importance in the development of Florentine painting. Indeed, the two other beautiful *Maestà* displayed on either side of this work, one by Cimabue and one by Duccio di Buoninsegna provide a vivid documentation of the background to Giotto's achievement (it is almost certain that as a young man he worked in Cimabue's workshop). The two earlier works (c 1285) mark a final development in the Byzantine style of painting, where a decorative sense still predominates, but Giotto's *Maestà*, painted about 25 years later heralds a new era in western painting. The figure of the Madonna acquires a striking monumentality and she is set in a more clearly defined space. The altarpiece was painted for the church of Ognissanti, but has been in the Uffizi since 1919.

Cimabue, *Maestà*

Duccio di Buoninsegna, *Maestà*

DUOMO

Polyptych

This is another very beautiful but badly damaged *Polyptych* by Giotto. It probably adorned the high altar of the church from about 1305 until 1520, but now it is kept in a chapel in the left apse at the east end of the church and is usually very difficult to see from close up. It is painted on both faces (the first such work known in Florence), and the back of it is the most interesting side and the best preserved, showing the *Annunciation*, and *Saints John the Baptist*, *Mary Magdalen*, *Reparata*, and *Nicholas*.

SANTA MARIA NOVELLA, OGNISSANTI, SAN FELICE IN PIAZZA

Crucifixes

Santa Maria Novella
Crucifix

Three monumental *Crucifixes* by Giotto also survive in three churches in Florence. One of them was removed for restoration in 1987 from the sacristy of Santa Maria Novella but has recently returned to the church where it hangs in the nave. It is an early work. The *Crucifix* in Ognissanti (1320), usually displayed in the sacristy, but at present removed for restoration, can be seen on request at the Cenacolo beside the church. It has a superb frame and although its attribution to Giotto has been doubted in the past, it is now usually recognized as an autograph work. The beautiful *Crucifix* in San Felice (close to Piazza Pitti) has recently been hung above the high altar, after its careful restoration. It is also interesting for its unusual iconography showing the pelican feeding her young, a symbol of the sacrifice of Christ (in the cimasa at the top), which was later much copied.

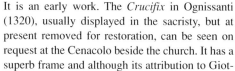

San Felice in Piazza
Crucifix

**MUSEO DIOCESANO
DI SANTO STEFANO
AL PONTE**

Madonna and Child

Two less important works in Florence represent Giotto's very earliest style and his very late style. The *Madonna and Child* from San Giorgio alla Costa (see picture above) may be his first work of all. However, it is very damaged, the throne reduced in size, and it has been much restored (only the two angels, the best preserved parts, reveal the high quality of the painting).

MUSEO HORNE

St Stephen

The painting of *St Stephen* is one of the most beautiful paintings by Giotto in Florence. It was once part of a polyptych (possibly one of the four painted for Santa Croce), and probably dates from around 1330 as it shows many similarities with the Bardi frescoes in that church. The gold ground was painted over a preparation of green paint.

VILLA I TATTI (Settignano)

Two small works almost unanimously assigned to Giotto are kept in the Villa I Tatti at Settignano just outside Florence. They were purchased by Bernard Berenson (1865-1959), the pioneer scholar of the Italian Renaissance, and form part of his private collection left to Harvard University. They represent a *Franciscan Saint* (or *St Anthony of Padua*), and the *Deposition*. The *Deposition* is one of seven beautiful small panels of the same size from an altar-frontal presumably painted for a Franciscan church (the others are now in museums in Boston, New York, Munich, and London).

**SANTA MARIA
A RICORBOLI**

Madonna and Child

This work is in a little known church rarely visited by tourists. It is on the south bank of the Arno in Via Benedetto Fortini, just off Viale Michelangelo. The painting hangs in the second north chapel. It is a very late but damaged work.

FILIPPO BRUNELLESCHI

Brunelleschi's architectural works carried out at the beginning of the 15th century were at once recognized as totally innovative. His buildings in Florence had rational clean lines following precise mathematical proportions, which were to influence architecture all over Europe for the next four centuries. Some elements of his architectural style were derived from ancient Roman works, Tuscan Romanesque churches, and, in the case of the cupola of the Duomo, from the Gothic arch. In the company of his friend the great sculptor Donatello he made several visits to Rome where he studied in detail the constructional techniques of the ancient Romans. Without his extraordinary engineering skills he would not have been able to erect his masterpiece, the huge dome of the Duomo.

Andrea Cavalcanti, called Buggiano, *Portrait of Brunelleschi*. Florence, Duomo

Born in Florence in 1377, he trained as a goldsmith and was also a very fine sculptor: he participated in the competition for the north door of the Baptistery in 1401 which is often taken as a convenient point to mark the beginning of the Florentine Renaissance. The competition was won by his rival Lorenzo Ghiberti, but the two artists remained closely linked for a while since the officials of the Opera del Duomo (the office responsible for the cathedral works) decided to appoint them jointly in 1418-20 to the task of vaulting the huge space (41 metres in diametre) over the drum of the cathedral. However by 1423 Brunelleschi was able to demonstrate that only he fully understood the technical problems involved and finally got the commission to complete the work on his own, and so produced one of the greatest architectural works of all time.

He also designed the two important churches of San Lorenzo and Santo Spirito, which both have simple harmonious interiors, with numerous classical references, and carefully worked out mathematical proportions. He built two beautiful little centrally-planned chapels: the Sagrestia Vecchia in San Lorenzo for the Medici, and an even more beautiful chapel beside Santa Croce for the Pazzi. He unfortunately never completed another interesting centrally planned work, the church of Santa Maria degli Angeli, the design of which was directly derived from classical buildings. Although very little civic architecture survives by him, and his design for Palazzo Medici (now lost) is known to have been rejected by Cosimo il Vecchio since he felt it was too grand, most scholars now believe Brunelleschi was responsible for the design of the original façade of Palazzo Pitti (which was later enlarged on both sides).

He used the dark grey pietra serena

quarried near Florence in many of his buildings to highlight architectural features, and also sought the collaboration of Donatello and the Della Robbia who provided decorative features such as tondoes in the spandrels of arches.

It is known that Brunelleschi experimented with perspective and the problem of representing a three-dimensional object on a flat surface, and was the first artist to apply its rules with a certain precision to architecture. He studied both mathematics and mechanics and recognized the importance of applying scientific principles to works of art, and in particular to architecture. He was the first person, probably with the help of the mathematician Evangelista Torricelli, to understand the rules of linear perspective inventing and putting to use the principle of the *camera obscura*. It could be said that without Brunelleschi's intuition in this field photography could not have been invented.

Numerous architectural backgrounds in Renaissance paintings and frescoes can be seen to be derived from Brunelleschi's architecture, and in particular the airy loggie he first invented for the arcaded façade of the Spedale degli Innocenti, and the cloisters inside the convent (which are a favourite feature of numerous representations of the Annunciation). The architectural setting for Masaccio's fresco of the *Trinity* in Santa Maria Novella is also recognized as being inspired directly by Brunelleschi's works, who may even have advised his friend Masaccio on the scientifically exact rules of linear perspective the younger artist adopted

Giorgio Vasari and Marco da Faenza, *Brunelleschi and Ghiberti presenting the Model for the Church of San Lorenzo to Cosimo il Vecchio.* Florence, Palazzo Vecchio

for this fresco restored in 2001.

Brunelleschi was extremely famous in his lifetime and after his death in 1446 he was the only Florentine allowed burial inside the cathedral. While the cupola was still being built, Leon Battista Alberti dedicated his remarkable treatise on painting (*De pictura*) to Brunelleschi, claiming that his works equalled and at times even surpassed those of the ancient Romans. Although no drawings or writings survive by Brunelleschi, we are able to get extraordinarily close to him since his death mask survives in the Museo dell'Opera del Duomo. His trial relief, along with that of Ghiberti, for the Baptistery competition is also preserved, as well as a wood model for the lantern of the cupola which most scholars consider must be by his own hand. In addition, a remarkable group of tools and apparatus apparently used during the construction of the cupola were found a few decades ago in a storeroom in the cathedral.

Ludovico Cigoli, detail from a drawing showing the Cupola. Florence, Gabinetto dei Disegni e delle Stampe degli Uffizi

DUOMO

The cupola

The most important of Brunelleschi's works, this was the largest and highest dome of its time. It was the first one to be projected without the need for a wooden supporting frame to sustain the vault during construction. This was partly possible because it was built with bricks laid in consecutive rings in horizontal courses, at intervals bonded together by bricks laid in a herring-bone pattern. It has two concentric shells, the outer one thinner than the inner one. Its pointed shape was conditioned by the octagonal drum which had already been built over the cross-

Detail of the constructional technique of the Cupola showing bricks laid in a herring-bone pattern

The staircase between the two shells of the Cupola

Brunelleschi's tomb

The simple tomb slab was found beneath the south aisle of the Duomo in 1972. In the church above is a medallion with a commemorative bust of Brunelleschi (probably taken from his death mask) by his adopted son Buggiano (1446), commissioned by the Opera del Duomo.

The north sacristy lavabo

This marble *lavabo* was carved by Buggiano, but was probably designed by Brunelleschi himself.

Details of the lantern designed by Brunelleschi

ing. However, the precise constructional technique has yet to be fully explained.

You can still climb up between the two shells along the staircases and corridors used by Brunelleschi and his workmen.

MUSEO DELL'OPERA DEL DUOMO

Bust of Brunelleschi

The bust attributed to Buggiano was probably commissioned for its present position, which was the former entrance to the headquarters of the Opera del Duomo.

Brunelleschi's death mask

This is a particularly moving work, showing the plain features of this great Florentine. It is a remarkable survival: the only other one which still exists in Florence from Renaissance times is that of Lorenzo il Magnifico which is exhibited in the Museo degli Argenti in Palazzo Pitti.

Tools and apparatus

The tools and apparatus probably used during the construction (or the maintenance) of the cupola have recently been arranged as in a building site, thought to be similar to the one set up by Brunelleschi during work on the cupola. They include pulleys, ropes, tackle, and hoists, and the original brick moulds. It is known that Brunelleschi was particularly able as a site manager, and understood the importance of organising his work force in the best possible way. He was apparently the first to institute the idea of a canteen for his workers.

Wooden model for the lantern

This model is thought to be the one made by Brunelleschi for the competition held in 1436 after he had completed work on the dome. It is astonishing that the great artist was subjected to yet another competition for this crowning element of the dome so essential to enhance its beautiful proportions. Although he won the competition, the lantern was only begun a few months before his death in 1446, but his friend Michelozzo completed it to his design.

Chiostro delle donne

This is the most beautiful part of the convent buildings designed by Brunelleschi (but later altered). Instead of the more usual quadrangular shape, the cloister is oblong which gives an even more interesting perspective view between the columns. It has 24 slender Ionic columns beneath a low loggia.

SPEDALE DEGLI INNOCENTI

The colonnade of the façade

O ne of his earliest works, this was commissioned from Brunelleschi by the Arte della Seta in 1419. Probably inspired by the nearby Loggia dell'Ospedale di San Matteo (now the Accademia di Belle Arti), built at the end of the 14th century, the nine semicircular arches have delightful medallions by Andrea della Robbia in the spandrels. This unique architectural feature was to be used often during the Renaissance and later. It was copied in this same piazza by Antonio da Sangallo the elder in the 16th century to complete the symmetry of the square and make it the most beautiful piazza in Florence.

SAN LORENZO

B runelleschi was commissioned by the Medici in 1425 to rebuild the church of San Lorenzo, probably the oldest in the city, which was only completely demolished in 1465. It became the burial place of all the principal members of the Medici family from Cosimo il Vecchio onwards. The cruciform plan is derived from early Christian and medieval churches such as Santa Croce, but the interior is one of the most beautiful works of the early Renaissance. The simple architectural features produce an extraordinary effect of harmony, and they are highlighted by the use of pietra serena. A very unusual element are the pronounced pulvins in pietra forte, between the Corinthian capitals and the spring of the arches. The space between the columns diminishes towards the east end to increase the perspective effect of the colonnade. The architectural details in the south transept, including the splendid Corinthian columns, are particularly fine, and were certainly completed by

Brunelleschi himself. Work on the church progressed slowly because of problems of funding, and the interior was only completed following the original designs in the second half of the 15th century by Antonio Ciacheri Manetti and Pagno di Lapo Portigiani.

Sagrestia Vecchia

The Sagrestia Vecchia was commissioned from Brunelleschi by Giovanni di Bicci de' Medici, father of Cosimo il Vecchio, who is buried here, and was the first part of San Lorenzo to be rebuilt. A simple quadrangular chapel with a beautiful vault, it is Brunelleschi's first centrally-planned building, a design which he later re-elaborated in the Cappella dei Pazzi and Santa Maria degli Angeli. The exquisite decorative details are by Donatello. The date 1428 which has recently been discovered on the lantern suggests it was completed by this time.

The second cloister

One of the most beautiful and peaceful spots in Florence, it is sometimes attributed to Brunelleschi, although it was only finished in 1453, after his death.

SANTA CROCE

Cappella dei Pazzi

The Cappella dei Pazzi is one of Brunelleschi's most famous works. It was commissioned as a chapter house and family chapel by the Pazzi in 1429/30, and develops the symmetrical architectural features of his earlier centrally planned chapel, the Sagrestia Vecchia in San Lorenzo. It has a remarkably serene and harmonious atmosphere. The rib-vaulted dome has little oculi which provide illumination, and in the pendentives of the cupola are polychrome roundels of the Evangelists, possibly also designed by Brunelleschi. The twelve roundels in enamelled terracotta of the seated Apostles are by Luca della Robbia. The portico was only completed in 1461 and is thought to have been designed by Giuliano da Maiano.

SANTA MARIA NOVELLA

Crucifix

The *Crucifix* in the Cappella Gondi is the only sculptural work to survive in wood by Brunelleschi. The story is told by Giorgio Vasari that Brunelleschi complained that Donatello's *Crucifix* in Santa Croce was a mere 'peasant on the Cross' and that he carved this work to show his friend how the Redeemer should be represented (it was obviously made to wear a loin-cloth).

Masaccio
Trinity

The fresco by Masaccio of the *Trinity* in the nave of the church makes use of a perspective device and an architectural background both of which show the influence of Brunelleschi. It is now thought the architect may have intervened directly to help Masaccio with its design.

SANTO SPIRITO

The interior of the church was designed by Brunelleschi but building was not begun until 1444 just two years before his death, and its construction continued for most of the 15th century, at first under the direction of his collaborator Antonio Manetti. Here Brunelleschi adopts a traditional Latin cross plan, but gives it a unique new design, with a dome over the crossing, and a continuous unbroken vaulted arcade which is carried right round the transepts and east end. The colonnade of 35 columns in pietra forte has Corinthian capitals with imposts above. In the perimeter walls there is also a continuous line of 38 chapels formed by semicircular niches. The effect of the

Palazzo di Parte Guelfa

Some architectural features designed by Brunelleschi for Palazzo di Parte Guelfa survive, including the windows of the great hall on the exterior, and the pilasters in the interior.
Palazzo Bardi alle Grazie (or Busini) at 5 Via dei Benci is also attributed to him.

simple architectural lines, based on mathematical proportions, and classical canons, is one of the greatest harmony. At the same time the details are more pronounced and sculptural than in his earlier church, San Lorenzo, and point the way forward to the more elaborate and less delicate 16th century style of architecture.

MUSEO NAZIONALE DEL BARGELLO

Sacrifice of Isaac

The trial relief for the competition for the second Baptistery doors is displayed next to Lorenzo Ghiberti's trial relief of the same subject. The reliefs were required to fit the Gothic quatrefoil frames. Although Ghiberti's relief was chosen, the decision was only reached by a narrow majority. But the course of artistic development in Florence was determined by the result, since it meant that Ghiberti went on to receive the commission for the third set of doors, his most celebrated work, which took him most of his life to complete, while Brunelleschi had time instead to devote himself to the problem of providing a dome to finish the cathedral.

Some of the details of his relief, such as the servant boy extracting a splinter from his foot reveal a close knowledge of Hellenistic Roman art (this figure was based on that of the *Spinario* in the Musei Capitolini, Rome). This is the only bronze sculptural work by Brunelleschi left in Florence: he trained as a goldsmith and some small bronzes made by him for the altar of St James can be seen in the cathedral of Pistoia.

Lorenzo Ghiberti, *Sacrifice of Isaac*. Florence, Museo Nazionale del Bargello

Hellenistic Roman sculpture, *Spinario*. Rome, Musei Capitolini

PALAZZO PITTI

The central part of the façade is attributed by most scholars to Brunelleschi, although no drawings of it survive. It was later greatly enlarged, but its appearance as designed by Brunelleschi may be similar to the detail in the predella of a painting by Alessandro Allori of *Martyred Saints* (1574) – see picture on the right – in a chapel at the east end of Santo Spirito.

Alessandro Allori, *Martyred Saints*, detail

ROTONDA DI SANTA MARIA DEGLI ANGELI

This was Brunelleschi's last and most sophisticated centrally-planned building based on ancient Roman models. However it is very difficult to appreciate since it was left unfinished and is now used as a language laboratory by Florence university. The first centrally-planned church building, it was to have a great influence on his successors who went on to produce some superb centrally-planned churches throughout Italy during the High Renaissance.

SANTA FELICITA

Cappella Capponi

It is known that Brunelleschi designed the Cappella Capponi (later frescoed by Pontormo), but the dome was subsequently lowered and so the proportions have been drastically altered.

MASACCIO

M asaccio was the most important painter of the early Renaissance who had a profound influence on his contemporaries. This is all the more remarkable since he died extremely young, probably at the age of 27. As Bernard Berenson stated "Masaccio, then, like Giotto a century earlier – himself the Giotto of an artistically more propitious world – was, as an artist, a great master of the signifi-cant, and, as a painter, endowed to the highest degree with a sense of tactile values, and with a skill in rendering them. In a career of but a few years he gave to Florentine painting the direction it pursued to the end." (*The Italian Painters of the Renaissance*, 1952).

Masaccio was born in 1401 near Florence in San Giovanni Valdarno, and his real name was Tommaso di Giovanni Cassai (his ancestors had been cabinet-makers, hence 'Cassai' from 'cassa', or chest). His father was an artisan who later became a notary but he died in 1406. It is probable that, together with his widowed mother and his brother, the painter Lo Scheggia, Masaccio moved to Florence in 1417. He may have entered the workshop of Bicci di Lorenzo, but he was at once struck by the works of Donatello and Brunelleschi and he was already known in Florence as a painter by

Masaccio and Filippino Lippi, *St Peter bringing back to Life the Son of Theophilus and St Peter Enthroned*, detail showing Masaccio's self-portrait. Florence, Santa Maria del Carmine

1419. His most famous works are the frescoes in the Cappella Brancacci in the church of the Carmine in Florence which were immediately recognized as a masterpiece. They combine a perfect application of the new rules of perspective with a remarkable use of chiaroscuro. They were closely studied by all his contemporaries in Florence and had a profound influence on the course of the Renaissance.

It is known that Masolino da Panicale, an experienced fresco painter who was also from the Valdarno, was Masaccio's master and he worked with him on the frescoes in the Brancacci chapel. The two artists also collaborated in the panel painting of the *Madonna and Child with St Anne*, now in the Uffizi. It is thought that they may have made a trip to Rome together in 1423. Masolino also worked for Cardinal Branda Castiglione in Rome (where he frescoed the chapel of St Catherine in San Clemente, possibly with the help of his pupil in some of these scenes) and in the little town of Castiglione Olona in Lombardy where he left his masterpieces in fresco before his death around 1440.

Masaccio's remarkable fresco of the *Trinity* in Santa Maria Novella which he probably painted a year before his death, is famous for its composition and accurate perspective, derived from Brunelleschi. The achievements of the young Masaccio were astounding to his contemporaries and his works were studied by many succeeding generations of artists: as Brunelleschi commented when he learned of his premature death (the circumstances of which are unknown): "*Noi habbiamo fatto una gran perdita*" [we have had a great loss].

Although it is in Florence that Masaccio can best be appreciated, works by him can also be seen in Pisa, Naples and Rome, and in museums in Berlin, Boston, London, and Washington.

Santa Maria del Carmine

Cappella Brancacci

To see the frescoes in the Cappella Brancacci you now enter through the peaceful cloister on the right of the church of Santa Maria del Carmine. The frescoes are extremely easy to examine in detail as they are not too high up on the walls and the illumination, mostly by natural light from a window on the altar wall, is excellent and not too bright.

The cycle illustrates the *Story of St Peter*. It was commissioned jointly from Masolino and Masaccio c 1424 by Felice Brancacci, a rich Florentine silk merchant and statesman. It is thought that the overall design of the fresco cycle is due to Ma-

solino who probably worked on the frescoes in 1425 before leaving for Hungary in the same year, and again in 1428 together with Masaccio who seems to have taken over full responsibility for them after Masolino's departure for Rome in 1429. Later that year Masaccio himself broke off work abruptly on the frescoes for an unknown reason, and left for Rome, where, by the end of the year, he had died. Brancacci was exiled from Florence in 1436 as an enemy of the Medici (he had married Palla Strozzi's daughter in 1431), and the cycle was only completed some 50 years later by Filippino Lippi who carefully integrated his style with that of Masaccio, possibly following an earlier design.

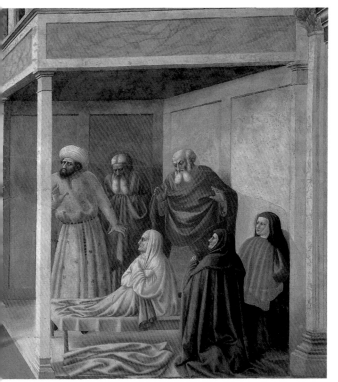

St Peter bringing Tabitha back to Life and healing a Lame Man, accompanied by St John, and detail

St Peter preaching

The frescoes are arranged in two registers. The upper scene on the entrance arch of the *Temptation of Adam and Eve* is by Masolino, who also executed the upper scene on the right wall of *St Peter bringing Tabitha back to Life and healing a Lame Man, accompanied by St John*. In the background is a charming view of Florence, and some of the details, including the two figures on the left, are sometimes attributed to Masaccio. On the altar wall the upper scene of *St Peter baptising the Neophytes* is by Masaccio. It is famous for its figure studies in the group of converts, including the strong young man kneeling before St Peter and the man in the background, just undressed, and shivering from the cold. The upper scene on the left of the altarpiece, of *St Peter preaching*, is by Masolino.

The upper scene on the left wall of the *Tribute Money* (as related in the gospel of St Matthew chapter 17, verse 24) is perhaps Masaccio's masterpiece. Three episodes are depicted in the same scene; in the centre, Christ surrounded by the Apostles, outside the gates of the city of Capernaum is asked by an official (with his back to us) to pay the tribute money owed to the city. Christ indicates a lake (the sea of Galilee) to St Peter, and (on the left) Peter is shown extracting the money from the mouth of a fish at the side of the lake. The scene on the right shows Peter handing over the tribute money to the official. The carefully worked out perspective, derived directly from experiments carried out by Brunelleschi, was calculated to project the observer into the scene from the actual space of the chapel itself. The head of Christ is thought by most scholars to be by Masolino, and it may be that Masaccio asked his master to paint it as a tribute to him. Sometimes the figure dressed in a sumptuous purple cloak on the right of the central group is taken to be a portrait of Felice Brancacci. The background with grey

St Peter baptising the Neophytes, and detail

mountains and a menacing sky above a desolate landscape is also superbly painted.

The *Expulsion from Paradise*, the upper scene on the entrance arch, is one of Masaccio's most moving works. It is known to have been painted in just four days, and both figures show the influence of classical sculpture.

In the lower register, the scene to the right on the entrance arch showing the *Release of St Peter from Prison* is by Filippino Lippi, who also painted the scene on the right wall of *Saints Peter and Paul before the Proconsul*, and the *Crucifixion of St Peter*. On the altar wall are two beautiful scenes by Masaccio of *Saints Peter and John distributing Alms* and *St Peter, followed by St John, healing the Sick with his Shadow*. The scene of *Saints Peter and John distributing Alms* incorporates the moving figure of a poor woman with her baby scantily dressed, one of the most memorable works produced by Masaccio. The dignified group of beggars around her are depicted with the same sensitivity. The scene includes the story of the death of Ananias (shown lying dead in the foreground) who had broken his vow to share his property with others. The cardinal kneeling in the background (half hidden) could be Cardinal Rainaldo or Cardinal Tommaso Brancacci. Beyond the houses of Florence is a charming glimpse of the hilly countryside on the outskirts of the town. In *St Peter healing the Sick with his Shadow*, the figure

The Tribute Money, and details

SANTA MARIA NOVELLA

Trinity

The other masterpiece by Masaccio in Florence is his fresco of the *Trinity* in Santa Maria Novella. It was rediscovered on the wall of the north aisle of the church in 1861 and detached. Its date is uncertain, although it was almost certainly executed between 1425 and 1428: formerly it was thought to have been commissioned by Domenico Lenzi for his altar here, but it now seems more likely to have been ordered by Fra' Alessio Strozzi, a cultivated theologian who was a close friend of both Ghiberti and Brunelleschi. It shows the figure of God the Father and Christ on the Cross in a shadowy barrel-vaulted niche, the architecture of which owes much to Brunelleschi, who was a friend of Masaccio's, and who may well have intervened in the design of the extremely accurate perspective. On either side are the striking figures of the Virgin and St John the Evangelist and the two donors. A skeleton lies on the painted altar below (this part of the fresco was only discovered in 1951). The fresco is famous for its perfect composition and for the remarkable equilibrium between the figures, almost sculptural in form, and the architecture. Indeed, it seems to suggest the possibility of a perfect union between the three arts of painting, sculpture and architecture, which was to be one of the leading principles of the Florentine Renaissance. It has an atmosphere which succeeds in portraying the mysterious concept of the Trinity.

GALLERIA DEGLI UFFIZI

Madonna and Child

Displayed here since 1973 is a very small panel, showing the three-quarter length Madonna tickling the Child under his chin. It has Antonio Casini's coat-of-arms on the back, who was created Cardinal in 1426. An undocumented work found in a private collection and first published in 1950 by

DONATELLO

onatello is of-
ten considered
the greatest
sculptor of all
time. This is not only because of his remarkable
technical ability in all materials, but also because he
succeeded as few others
have ever done in portraying numerous aspects of the
human character. He was
the first sculptor to study
carefully and fully appreciate the qualities of ancient

17th century Florentine
painter, *Portrait of Donatello.*
Florence, Galleria degli Uffizi

Roman art. In his very long life he produced many masterpieces, the attribution
of some of which remains one of the
great art historical debates to this day.
His bibliography is more extensive than
that of any other artist of his century. He
carried out public commissions in Florence (in particular for the Opera del
Duomo) as well as working for private
patrons, but it was above all due to Cosimo il Vecchio de' Medici that from 1434
onwards he was able to work without
hindrance and protected from economic
worries. The two men became close
friends and it was Cosimo's wish that the
sculptor be buried beside him in the crypt
of San Lorenzo when he died just two
years before his protégé. Nearly all Donatello's greatest works made in Florence have remained here.

Donatello di Niccolò di Betto Bardi,
born in 1386 or 1387, came from a mod-
est family (his father was a wool-carder)
and it is probable that he always had dif-

ficulty in reading and writ-
ing. But even so, as his
works show, he was able to
absorb the neoplatonic theories and Humanist ideas of
the Renaissance and was
one of the leading figures in
that remarkable cultural and
artistic movement for which
Florence became famous
throughout the world.

As a young man he
was an assistant in Lorenzo
Ghiberti's workshop while
Ghiberti, eight years his
senior, was at work on the first set of
doors for the Baptistery. He then became
a great friend of the architect Brunelleschi and some of his earliest sculptures show the influence of Brunelleschi's statuettes made for an altar in
Pistoia and his trial relief for the Baptistery doors. In the first years of the 15th
century the two friends went to Rome to
study ancient Roman art which was to
have a fundamental influence on their
work. By the 1420s both men were highly esteemed by their contemporaries as
the greatest living architect and sculptor
in Florence. In his 'stiacciato' or 'schiacciato' reliefs Donatello was the first to
interpret Brunelleschi's theories of linear
perspective in sculpture, by emphasiz-
ing the delicate line in very low relief,
rather than the depth of the panel. It is
possible Brunelleschi intervened in the
design of Donatello's tabernacle on the
exterior of Orsanmichele for the Parte
Guelfa, and they certainly later collabo-

rated in the decoration of the Sagrestia Vecchia, and possibly also the Cappella Pazzi. When carving his *Mary Magdalen* Donatello may have been influenced by Brunelleschi's statue of Mary Magdalen in Santo Spirito which was destroyed by fire in 1471. Donatello was also a friend of Leon Battista Alberti and almost certainly went with him on a second trip to Rome.

Vasari tells the delightful story that when Donatello had finished his *Crucifix* (now in Santa Croce) he was so pleased with it that he showed it to Brunelleschi for his opinion. But when the architect saw it he complained that he had portrayed a mere peasant on the Cross. Donatello, highly disappointed, retorted that he would like to see Brunelleschi make a better one. Unbeknownst to anyone, Brunelleschi then proceeded to carve a Crucifix himself, and after some months, when he had finished it, he invited Donatello to his house for lunch. On their way, they did some shopping in the Mercato Vecchio and Brunelleschi gave the food to Donatello and told him to go ahead to his house and he would catch him up shortly. There Donatello found the Crucifix and was so impressed that he dropped the eggs and cheese and other food they had bought which he was carrying in his overalls. At that moment Brunelleschi entered, and laughing asked him how he thought they were going to eat now that he had let everything fall to the floor. Donatello replied that he had had his fill already for that day and that evidently Brunelleschi had been made to carve figures of Christ, and he figures of peasants!

As a sculptor Donatello was unusual in being able to use any material with equal ability, including bronze, marble, wood, limestone, terracotta, and stucco, although he sought the help of professional bronze-workers to cast his statues. His very low (*stiacciato*) reliefs explored the pictorial possibilities of sculpture in a way that had never been experimented before. Many of his works were painted and gilded by his own hand. No drawings which can definitely be attributed to him survive. Donatello was always extremely careful to take into account the

viewpoint of the spectator, and many of his works were 'distorted' so that their proportions were exact when seen from a certain distance: the arrangement of some of his works today in the museums of the Opera del Duomo (the *St John the Evangelist* and the Campanile statues) and the Bargello (the bronze *David*) are mistakenly displayed too low. The heads of his sculptures often have classical features, but also contain portraits of his contemporaries, presumably made from life models. Vasari recounts that while Donatello was working on *Habbakuk* for the campanile, he looked him full in the face and ordered him to speak: "*Favella, favella, ..!*". Indeed, to this day his sculptures seems to possess every quality except that of speech.

Donatello was also remarkably skilled in rendering clothing, from tight fitting rigid armour, to long flowing 'Baroque' robes. He showed great sensitivity in creating architectural settings for some of his sculptures (such as the monument in the Baptistery, the *Cavalcanti Annunciation*, the Sagrestia Vecchia, the Orsanmichele tabernacles).

His *David* was the first nude freestanding life-size sculpture in bronze since antiquity, and his *Judith* was the first sculpture since Roman times to explore the possibilities of a statuary group depicting an action about to take place. Both these extraordinary allegorical statues are known to have been in the garden of Palazzo Medici, and they were confiscated by the Signoria after the expulsion of the Medici in 1495 and moved to Palazzo Vecchio. Vasari in 1568 summed up the effect his statues had on his contemporaries (and the effect they still have for us today) when he described his *St George*: "fully armed and most lively; in the head we see the beauty of youth, the spirit and pride of arms, and a terrible ardour. Life itself seems to be stirring marvellously within the stone. And certainly in the statues of modern times no such liveliness has been seen, nor such spirit in marble, as nature and art here achieved by the hand of Donatello ".

Donatello established a large workshop in Florence, which thrived especially from 1428 until he left for Padua, where he carried out the only important commissions he ever accepted outside of Florence (the *Altar* of the Basilica of Il Santo and the *Equestrian Statue of Gattamelata*). Through these works Donatello introduced the art of the Florentine Renaissance into northern Italy. It is known that Bertoldo (who was later to have an important influence on the young Michelangelo) and Bartolomeo Bellano both worked with him as assistants. Donatello's most intelligent pupil was Desiderio da Settignano, some of whose works have formerly been attributed to his master. Donatello was apparently not a very practical person and had difficulty in keeping his accounts and administering his money. From around 1424 for a period of some years he worked in association with the architect and sculptor and caster of bronze Michelozzo, who it seems also helped him with his administrative problems. Together they produced the splendid *Monument to the Antipope John XXIII* in the Baptistery (and they also collaborated in the Sagrestia Vecchia in San Lorenzo).

The elderly Cosimo il Vecchio stipulated in his will that his son should look after the aged sculptor. To this end Piero gave Donatello a small farm at Cafaggiuolo, but after just one year the sculptor returned it to the Medici complaining that it caused him too much trouble with administration! Piero apparently took this in good humour as he supplied him with a life pension instead. Vasari also tells the touching story that when Donatello, who had never married, was ill and close to death at the end of his life, he was visited by his relations who asked him to leave them a farm he owned in Prato. The sculptor, however, refused, telling them that the peasant who had worked on it all his life had a much more legitimate claim to it, and he at once saw to it, through a notary, that it went instead to him.

Many of his works in Florence, including *Judith* and the decorative details in the Sagrestia Vecchia have been carefully restored in recent years. His only important works still awaiting restoration and detailed study are the bronze panels on the two *Pulpits* in San Lorenzo which were his last and perhaps most moving works of all, in which the scenes from the Passion of Christ show a highly personal interpretation and a new departure from traditional iconography. He worked on these up until his death at the age of 80, and his funeral in Florence, attended by nearly the whole city, was the most splendid tribute paid to any Florentine artist before Michelangelo's elaborate funeral service in San Lorenzo.

As one of the greatest scholars of Renaissance sculpture John Pope-Hennessy so aptly stated Donatello's works are "messages transmitted by posterity by one of the most purposeful, most human, and most self-revealing artists who has ever lived".

Donatello, *St George and the Dragon*. Florence, Museo Nazionale del Bargello

BAPTISTERY

Monument to the Antipope John XXIII

Baldassarre Coscia, who had close connections with Florence, and through whom the Medici became papal bankers, was elected Pope during the great Schism in 1410. He was expelled from Rome by Imperial troops and fled to Florence in 1413. He was deposed the following year by a council in Constance and immediately imprisoned. Through his Florentine connections he was finally released in 1419 on condition he recognized Martin V Colonna as his legitimate successor. He returned to Florence and died in the same year. Giovanni di Bicci de' Medici and Niccolò da Uzzano (whose portrait Donatello later sculpted) were among the executors of his will and since he had asked to be buried in the Baptistery it was they who in

1424 commissioned Donatello and Michelozzo to produce his funerary monument, one of the earliest Renaissance tombs in the city. It is especially remarkable for the way it is inserted into the narrow space between two huge Roman columns and in no way disturbs the architectural harmony of this greatly revered historic building. It is thought that Donatello intervened in the design of the monument as well as carving the splendid gilded bronze effigy of the Pope and some of the sculptural details. The effigy, a portrait of the pope, perhaps taken from a death mask, was probably cast by Michelozzo. The cushion, embroidered robes, and drapes are superbly decorated. The statues in niches and the relief of the Madonna and Child are, instead, by Michelozzo and his workshop.

DUOMO

Coronation of the Virgin

This east window with the *Coronation of the Virgin* in the drum of the cupola is the most important of the seven beautiful stained glass roundels designed in 1434 by leading artists of the day (the others are by Paolo Uccello, Andrea del Castagno and Lorenzo Ghiberti), and made after Brunelleschi had completed the cupola. Donatello's window is unfortunately very damaged and has lost a lot of its colour, but its circular monumental design is remarkable. These windows, the glass for which came from Venice, are among the most important works of their kind ever made in Italy.

Joshua (attributed)

This statue on the first altar on the north side of the nave is almost certainly derived from a model by Donatello. It is traditionally thought to be a portrait of the humanist friend of Cosimo il Vecchio, Poggio Bracciolini. Probably destined for the campanile, it was first commissioned from Bernardo Ciuffagni, then in 1418 Donatello was asked to complete it and make a substitute head, but he passed it on to his collaborator Nanni di Bartolo who finished it in 1421.

Museo dell'Opera del Duomo

Cantoria

T he so-called *Cantoria*, or singing gallery, was instead made as an organ loft, as a pair with the one displayed opposite by Luca della Robbia, which were to be placed above the two sacristy doors in the Duomo. They were dismantled and partly destroyed in 1688, and the upper frieze was then reconstructed, and some of the architectural features replaced in 1841 by Gaetano Baccani. Donatello received the commission in 1433 after his second trip to Rome and it shows the influence of Roman sculpture. The remarkable frieze of dancing putti which are derived from Roman sarcophagus reliefs, against a background of coloured mosaic inlay shows Donatello's ingenuity in producing a highly decorative panel.

St John the Evangelist

T his seated statue was Donatello's first large-scale statue, dating from 1408. It is one of four statues (the others, still very Gothic in spirit, are by Nanni di Banco, Bernardo Ciuffagni, and Niccolò di Pietro Lamberti) made for the old façade of the cathedral. They were designed to fit the shallow niches on either side of the central doorway, and are therefore really very high reliefs and not sculptures fully in the round. The upper part of the body is elongated to account for its raised position about three metres above ground (it is now displayed lower than it was originally intended). The forceful features reveal a close understanding of ancient Roman sculpture. After the façade was demolished in 1587, the statues were housed inside the Duomo, and then moved to the museum in 1936.

Bearded Prophet

This is one of a series of statues commissioned from Donatello for the niches in the Campanile which had been left empty since the 14th century. The niches are some 15 metres above ground level, and the statues were carefully designed by Donatello to take this into account and all of them peer meditatively downwards at the spectator in the square below: at present they are mistakenly displayed at eye level. They were moved to the museum in the 1930s by which time they were extremely badly damaged, and it is now difficult to appreciate the quality of the marble carving because of their poor condition. It is almost certain that Donatello made a life-size model in clay or plaster before beginning work on this statue.

Beardless Prophet

Also made for a niche in the Campanile, this is Donatello's first statue in which he provides a portrait, apparently modelled on a wax or clay head. Although the prophet has markedly classical features, at the time it was made it was presumed to be a portrait of one of Donatello's contemporaries, possibly Brunelleschi.

Abraham and Isaac

This was commissioned jointly from Donatello and Nanni di Bartolo for the Campanile, but it is generally considered that the very original composition of this two figure group is due to Donatello, who may have been influenced by the similar figures by Brunelleschi in his trial relief for the Baptistery doors. The figure of Isaac and the head of Abraham are thought to be largely the work of Nanni di Bartolo.

Jeremiah

Although also in very bad condition, this Campanile statue also has a remarkable portrait head, and is one of Donatello's most important marble sculptures. Here, as John Pope-Hennessy has pointed out, the statue produces the effect of a figure completely in the nude over which a heavy cloak has been thrown, almost by chance, as if the nude body beneath was considered separately from the clothes which cover it (an attitude which was later developed by Baroque sculptors). The identification of the statue with the prophet Jeremiah is conjectural, and in the 16th century there was a tradition that this statue and Habbakuk were portraits of two enemies of the Medici, Giovanni Chiericini and Francesco Soderini.

Habbakuk ('lo Zuccone')

This is another particularly fine work by Donatello for the Campanile, unfortunately very damaged. It has been undergoing restoration for some years and is not at present on view. Again Donatello uses a classical dress to accentuate rather than hide the emaciated nude body beneath. In the 15th and 16th centuries this was one of Donatello's most admired works, and the subject of Vasari's story that Donatello was found one day in his studio looking intensely at Habbakuk and commanding him to talk! Its nickname of 'lo Zuccone' or 'big-head' was already in use by the mid 16th century. The form of the skull indicates that the sculptor almost certainly used a life model, perhaps a retarded man, and it may be that Donatello therefore wished to suggest that wisdom, a gift from God, is in no way connected to one's physical aspect (a remarkably 'modern' idea, opposed to the classical concept of ideal beauty representing all that is best in mankind).

Jonah or St John the Baptist (attributed)

Although the inscription on the base bears the name of Donatello, the attribution of this work, also very damaged, is uncertain. It is also possible that it was at first destined for the façade of the Duomo and then moved to the Campanile. The head was carved separately, probably by Donatello himself, whereas the rest of the figure is probably only on a model by him.

Donatello, *St John the Baptist*. Venice, Santa Maria Gloriosa dei Frari

Mary Magdalen

This remarkable wood statue of the penitent Magdalen as an old toothless woman with only her long hair covering her nakedness and her hands seeming to shake as she attempts to join them in prayer is one of Donatello's most dramatic works. A late work, probably carved around 1454, it seems it may have been inspired by a statue in Santo Spirito by Brunelleschi also of the *Magdalen* which was lost in a fire in the late 15th century. It has similarities with Donatello's *St John the Baptist* in Venice, which is now thought to date from around 1438. The *Magdalen* was presumably carved for the Baptistery where it is documented for the first time in 1500, and it remained there, in a much more fitting setting, until it had to be restored after damage in the Arno flood in 1966. At that time the original gilding was discovered on its surface. Its present display, since the recent rearrangement of this museum, is particularly inappropriate.

Creation of Eve (attributed)

This small hexagonal glazed terracotta relief has recently been displayed in the museum in the room devoted to sculpture from the doors of the Cathedral and attributed to Donatello. It is instead probably part of a lost dowry chest, and its companion with three scenes from Genesis, now belongs to the Victoria and Albert Museum in London. It is particularly interesting as it may possibly have been an experiment (apparently never again repeated) in applying a transparent glaze to terracotta, as in ceramics (probably intended to be subsequently gilded). This would indicate that Donatello or an artist in his circle was already thinking about the possibilities of applying a more durable outer film to terracotta works, before Luca della Robbia perfected the technique of glazing enamelled terracottas.

Prophet from the Porta della Mandorla (attributed)

This small statue of a prophet was a pair with the one displayed beside it by Nanni di Banco made for the pinnacles of the tympanum of the Porta della Mandorla. It is usually considered one of Donatello's earliest works made when he was employed in the Opera del Duomo workshop. They were probably moved to the east door of the Campanile in 1431.

**Tabernacle of the
Armaiuoli**
(or *Corazzai e Spadai*)

The armourers guild
commissioned this
tabernacle and the
statue of *St George*
from Donatello. The
niche, shallower than
the others as there is a
spiral staircase in the
corner of the building
here, has a relief of
God the Father in the
tympanum. The statue
of *St George* was
replaced with a bronze
copy by Oronzio Lelli
when it was moved to
the Bargello in 1892,
and the original bas-
relief in the predella
has also been housed
in the Bargello since
its removal in 1976

ORSANMICHELE

Tabernacle of the Parte Guelfa

This, the largest taber-
nacle on the exterior
of Orsanmichele, was
commissioned from Don-
atello by the Parte Guelfa
together with a statue of
their patron saint St Louis
of Toulouse, which is now
in the Museo dell'Opera di
Santa Croce. It has classical elements including
Corinthian pilasters and
Ionic columns and a niche
in the shape of a scallop
shell. Other features de-
rived from Roman sar-
cophagi include the two
putti bearing a garland,
and the doubled sided
heads on the corners. In the tympanum is the Trinity symbol-
ized by three heads. It is thought by some scholars that
Brunelleschi may have been responsible for the design of the
tabernacle, although the delicate carved details are all by Donatello's own hand. In the mid 15th century the Parte Guelfa
sold the tabernacle to the Tribunale della Mercanzia and the
statue of *St Louis* was removed to Santa Croce. The present
bronze group which fills the niche is a copy of the *Incredulity
of St Thomas* commissioned by the Mercanzia from Verrocchio
in 1473.

MUSEO DI ORSANMICHELE

St Mark

This statue was commissioned in 1411
by the linen merchants and used
clothes dealers (*Linaioli* and *Rigattieri*),
and finished by 1413. It was damaged in
the 1920s but since its restoration in
1986 it has been replaced on the exterior
of the building by a copy. The proportions of the upper part of the body have
been carefully elongated to allow for its
raised position, and it was partly gilded.
One of Donatello's earliest works, the figure, made to stand in a very shallow niche,
has a classical head and pose.

PALAZZO VECCHIO

Judith and Holofernes

A masterpiece in bronze, this is one of Donatello's last and most sophisticated works, possibly commissioned by the Medici. Judith is shown in the act of decapitating Holofernes who sprawls, drunk, at her feet. The triangular base, decorated with reliefs symbolizing drunkenness, is particularly ingenious, with Holofernes' feet dangling over it, and the statue is designed to be seen from numerous different viewpoints. The heroine shows an expression of both determination and disgust for the act she is about to commit.

Dating from about 1454, there are holes at the corners of the cushion so the statue group appears to have been designed as a fountain. The scimitar and beautiful embroidered dress of Judith were gilded. It is known that the statue was in the courtyard of Palazzo Medici where it had an inscription which explained its allegorical significance as the victory of Humility over Pride. After the expulsion of the Medici in 1495 it was expropriated by the republican government and placed under the Loggia della Signoria with a new base and inscription warning against tyrants. Since its restoration it has been replaced in situ with a copy and removed to the Sala dei Gigli in Palazzo Vecchio.

SAN LORENZO

Decorative details in the Sagrestia Vecchia

This is one of Brunelleschi's lovely centrally-planned chapels built for Giovanni di Bicci de' Medici. The vault is particularly beautiful, and was completed in 1428, and some years later the architect's friend Donatello added the decoration to the eight tondi in the lunettes and pendentives showing the four *Evangelists* and *Scenes from the Life of St John the Evangelist*. The *Scenes from the Life of St John the Evangelist*, the iconography of three of which is inspired by the frescoes of the same subjects by Giotto in Santa Croce, are modelled in terracotta and plaster and are remarkable for their composition and narrative quality. Donatello here experimented with the technique used for stucco work by the ancient Romans, and produced extraordinary spatial effects in these four concave roundels. Probably with the help of Brunelleschi, he carefully studied the problems of perspective created by the fact that they are some 12 metres above the floor. The painted reliefs had to be modelled while the plaster was still wet and so here, as in no other work by Donatello, can we appreciate his working method and the immediacy with which he modelled each figure by hand (during restoration work his finger prints were even detected in places). They were spectacularly restored in 1989 so that all the details can again be appreciated.

Donatello used this technique only in these works, and they were never imitated, partly because a few years later Luca della Robbia invented glazed terracotta which was then widely used to decorate the tondoes in Brunelleschi's architecture.

Scenes from the Life of St John the Evangelist

St John on Patmos
Raising of Drusiana
Martyrdom of St John
Ascension of St John

The four Evangelists

Page 56: *Raising of Drusiana*, detail

The tondoes of the four *Evangelists* are, instead, on a flat plane, and their composition seems to have been derived from a Byzantine manuscript in the Medici library. Each of the saints has a portrait head rather than an idealized character. Below the vault is a frieze of cherubs' heads, presumably designed by Donatello, and above the two little doors are fine large reliefs of four saints which, however, are extraneous elements in the context of Brunelleschi's architecture (and it seems that Brunelleschi complained about them). The extremely delicate relief of *Saints Lawrence and Stephen* on the left is usually attributed to Donatello's own hand, whereas that of the Medici saints *Cosmas and Damian* is thought to be the work of his collaborator Michelozzo. The bronze doors beneath have remarkable reliefs of paired male figures, which for centuries were both thought to be by Donatello, but in recent years scholars have suggested that the one on the right with the *Apostles*, *Evangelists*, *St John the Baptist*, and the four *Fathers of the Church* may instead be by Michelozzo. The left door panels show philosophers and theologians in animated discussion and are remarkable for the number of different attitudes which are portrayed. Again it seems that the iconographical source for these scenes comes from a Byzantine manuscript.

Bust of St Lawrence (or ***St Leonard***)

This striking terracotta, displayed on a bench here, once thought to be by Donatello, is now usually considered to be by his pupil Desiderio da Settignano who may also have carved the lavabo decorated with exquisite fantastic creatures in the adjoining chapel.

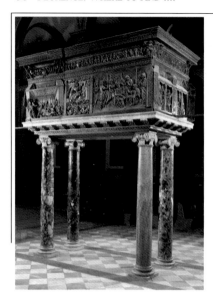

The two Pulpits

The bronze panels on these two pulpits are known to have been Donatello's last works, and he was at work on them up to the time of his death, with the help of four assistants. They depict the Passion of Christ and are extremely moving works, showing the universal tragedy of these events using an iconography quite new to western art. The grim crowded scenes portray an intense suffering. However, they are very difficult to examine in detail as they are some metres above ground in the dark nave of the church.

It is now thought that some of the superb panels of the north pulpit were intended for the former high altar of the church: they portray the *Maries at the Sepulchre, Resurrection, Christ in Limbo* and *Ascension*. It has been suggested that the iconog-

Page 59: *Christ before Pilate*

Martyrdom of St Lawrence

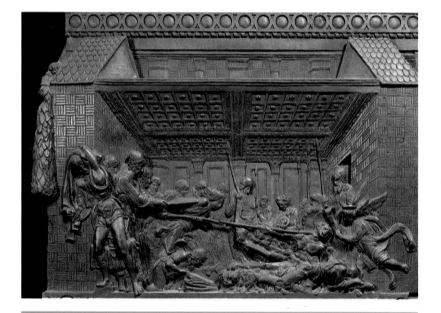

Sarcophagus of Niccolò and Fioretta Martelli (attributed)

This unusual tomb is in the form of a wicker basket. It has for long been attributed to Donatello since he is known to have frequented the Martelli family who were also his patrons, and Vasari attributed it to him, but it now appears that it was commissioned instead in 1463 or 1464 by Niccolò and Fioretta's son, Roberto, from Desiderio da Settignano. One of the handles is a restoration, but the original was found by chance in a private collection in 2000 and is to be returned.

raphy for the *Christ in Limbo* could have been taken from the exquisite Byzantine diptych in miniature mosaic which was made in Constantinople in the early 14th century and brought to Florence in the last years of the same century (it is now in the Museo dell'Opera del Duomo). The scene of the *Pentecost*, although designed by Donatello, was possibly not carved by his own hand. The *Martyrdom of St Lawrence* has a remarkable sense of depth and carefully worked out perspective.

It has recently been recognized that some of the scenes on the south pulpit are probably not by Donatello: the *Prayer in the Garden* and *Crucifixion* are attributed to Bartolomeo Bellano, and the *Deposition* to Bertoldo. But the other panels on this pulpit are very fine works by Donatello: the *Mourning over the Dead Christ* (which may include a portrait of Cosimo de' Medici in the figure just above the head of the Madonna), *Christ before Pilate* and *Christ before Caiaphas*. The panels were apparently not assembled in the church until 1515, so some time after Donatello's death, and they were probably raised on the present Ionic columns around 1560 and installed in their present position only in the 17th century when *St John the Evangelist* and the *Flagellation* on the south pulpit, and the *St Luke* and the *Mocking of Christ*, on the north pulpit, were made as imitations in wood. The autograph panels on the two pulpits are the only important works by Donatello in Florence still awaiting restoration and careful study.

Monument to Donatello

Donatello is buried in the vaults of the church and this monument by Dario Guidotti and Raffaello Romanelli was set up to commemorate him in the north transept of the church in 1896.

MUSEO NAZIONALE DEL BARGELLO

The Marzocco Lion

This heraldic lion, the symbol of the Republic of Florence, is displayed in the centre of the Sala del Consiglio Generale which contains the masterpieces of Donatello. Made in gray sandstone, it was commissioned from Donatello to decorate a staircase built in honour of Pope Martin V's visit to Florence in 1419 when he stayed in the convent of Santa Maria Novella. When the staircase was demolished in 1515 the lion must have been put in store since it reappeared again in the early 19th century when it was moved to outside Palazzo Vecchio to replace a 13th century lion. Later in the same century it was re-moved to the Bargello, since the stone is not suitable to be exposed in the open air.

St George

Crucifixion

A small gilded relief, this has recently been recognized by most scholars as by Donatello's hand (it was formerly usually attributed to his workshop). It is a very intricate composition with the main figures in high relief and extensive use of gilding on the armour and clothing of the protagonists. It may date from around 1454 and it is known that it was owned by the Medici.

This has always been one of the most admired statues by Donatello showing the saint as the young Champion of Christendom. By endowing the statue with a sense of move-ment, Donatello here resolves the difficult problem of placing a static figure within a niche, but at the same time not letting it appear to be confined. It is all the more striking since it is com-paratively small for its setting. An early work dating from about 1416, the remarkably well-composed statue, with an ideal sense of proportion, was at once recognized as a new departure from Gothic forms, and had a great influence on later sculptors. Donatello observed with extraordinary precision the delicate features of a very young man, as can be seen in the careful mod-elling of the mouth.

It was the first statue to be removed from the exterior of Or-sanmichele in 1892 when the tabernacle was reconstructed here. It was commissioned by the guild of armourers and Donatello was extremely careful to depict every de-tail of the saint's armour, probably copied from a real suit supplied by the guild. The beautiful bas-relief be-low of *St George and the Dragon* was removed from Orsanmichele in 1974 and carefully restored in 1982. It is a remarkable work in low relief (using the *schiacciato* technique) where for the first time Donatello shows an in-terest in linear perspective and picto-rial space. Both the figure of the princess and the particularly remark-able St George on horseback show the influence of classical sculpture.

David, statue in bronze

D avid is shown standing victorious over the severed head of Goliath, with its elaborate helmet lying on a laurel wreath. One of the most beautiful statues of the Renaissance it was the earliest free-standing nude to be made in bronze since Roman times.

Donatello here invented a new concept in sculpture in which the silhouette produced by the dark bronze is its most important feature. The unusual dark patina, which makes it look almost as if it was made of black marble, is so beautiful that it might even be the original one which Donatello gave it.

It was probably made between 1430 and 1440 for the Medici, but scholars are not agreed on its precise date. On their expulsion from Florence in 1495 it was moved, together with Donatello's *Judith*, to Palazzo della Signoria. The footwear and the peasant's hat, both of which recall the attributes of Mercury, have led some scholars to suggest the statue was meant to represent Mercury rather than David. However Donatello's choice to portray the young David nude follows closely the biblical story in the *Book of Samuel* where he is described as complaining that the armour that Saul had given him was too heavy and so he shed it before his famous fight with the giant. It has a strongly symbolic significance, suggesting that no protection is needed beyond that of God alone to overcome the most difficult of undertakings. It had an inscription when in Palazzo Medici exhorting the citizens of Florence to victory. Most statues of David made after this one, including Michelangelo's famous one, portrayed the hero nude.

It used to stand on a column and that is why David is looking sharply downwards, and so it should therefore be seen from below. It is thought there used to be a feather in David's cap as well as at the summit of Goliath's helmet. The relief on the helmet probably represents an allegory of the Triumph of Pride.

David, statue in marble

O̱ne of Donatello's earliest works this is far different in spirit to his later bronze statue of the same subject. It was commissioned by the Signoria for the Sala dell'Orologio in Palazzo Vecchio around 1412, probably to stand against a wall. It therefore has a frontal viewpoint, but was also carefully calculated to be seen from each side. It stood on a base nearly 2 metres high. The stone by which David killed Goliath can be seen embedded in his forehead. In 1781 the statue was moved to the Uffizi and about one hundred years later installed in the Bargello.

Frightened Man

This small bronze was first attributed to Donatello by Pope-Hennessy in the 20th century. He thought it may have represented a boxer, and recognized that it also had the same pose as one of the Roman figures of the *Dioscuri* on the Quirinal hill in Rome. He found similarities in the expression of the face to that of Donatello's statue of *Jeremiah*. The idea of making small bronzes, which had been produced in great numbers in Roman times, was reintroduced in the Renaissance period, as the great quantity of similar statues in this room demonstrates, and therefore if this attribution is correct it may be that this was the very first small bronze to be produced of the Renaissance.

Bust of Niccolò da Uzzano

Ṯhis remarkable coloured terracotta portrait, full of character, seems to have been the first Renaissance portrait bust; it was to be followed by numerous splendid busts (usually in marble) by other 15th century Florentine sculptors wich provided vivid portraits of their contemporaries. Although for long thought to be by Donatello, art historians in the 20th century tended to reject this traditional attribution. It was only after its careful restoration in 1985 that it has been almost universally accepted again as the work of Donatello himself. It was modelled on a living cast, using two moulds, and the anatomical details such as the neck and lips are extraordinary. It is one of the most memorable portraits in the city. Niccolò was a banker and learned ambassador who built Palazzo Capponi delle Rovinate on Via de' Bardi. On his death in 1432 the property went to his daughter's husband's family, the Capponi, who kept the bust in their palace until 1881 when it was moved to the Bargello.

Atys-Amorino

An enigmatic bronze work, it is uncertain what the allegorical significance of this mythological statue was meant to be. It portrays a young boy or winged faun with his feet lightly touching the ground entangled in a serpent and his arms raised, dressed in very strange (and unnecessary!) trousers. It is thought he may have once held a serpent in his hands.

It has been suggested that it could be a humorous allusion to the difficulties of love-making, with homosexual overtones, made at a time when it was fashionable amongst the male population to be in love with young men.

It has an engaging spirit, and may have been modelled for a fountain. It is known that it was owned by Angelo Doni, later patron of both Raphael and Michelangelo. In the 17th century it was taken for an ancient Roman work, possibly representing Mercury or Bacchus.

Martelli coat-of-arms

This was acquired by the State in 1998 from Palazzo Martelli as a work by Donatello, and installed here, although not all scholars agree with this attribution, some of whom suggest it may instead be an early work by his most gifted pupil, Desiderio da Settignano (who is also thought to have sculpted the Martelli tomb in San Lorenzo). It is a very beautiful coat-of-arms, partly gilded, but was repainted in the 19th century. Vasari recounts that Donatello frequented the Martelli household (very wealthy supporters of the Medici), and that they were also amongst his patrons.

Other beautiful works in the Sala del Consiglio Generale which are sometimes attributed to Donatello include the *Martelli Young St John the Baptist* (now recognized as a work by Desiderio da Settignano), the statuette of a *Dancing Putto*, the bronze *Bust of a Youth with a Medallion at his Neck*, and the head of a *Marine Divinity*.

Santa Croce

Cavalcanti Tabernacle of the Annunciation

This is a very unusual high relief of the *Annunciation* in a tabernacle which was part of the funerary monument of Niccolò Cavalcanti. It stood beside the choir screen of the church which was removed in the 16th century. It is made of limestone and there is a remarkable spiritual bond between the Virgin and Angel of the Annunciation which makes this one of

Filippo Lippi,
Annunciation, detail.
Florence, San Lorenzo

Right: *Annunciation*,
detail

CAPPELLA PAZZI

Four Evangelists

It has recently been suggested that it was Donatello rather than Brunelleschi who designed these lovely tondoes in enamelled terracotta for the cupola of this little chapel. They were then executed in Andrea della Robbia's workshop using an unusual number of bright colours. They are remarkably sophisticated works, and the use of so many colours, technically very complicated, was hardly ever used again.

For a description of the chapel, one of Brunelleschi's most important works, see p. 24.

Donatello's most deeply moving works. The architecture of the tabernacle and the background are intriguing and show the influence of Leon Battista Alberti, and the decorative scroll motifs on the tympanum were to be copied many times by Donatello's followers especially Michelozzo (see his tabernacle in San Miniato al Monte). The two figures are derived from classical models, and their poses appear to be influenced by Filippo Lippi's painting of the *Annunciation* in San Lorenzo.

Standing on the top of the tabernacle are six delightful terracotta putti, unfortunately very damaged, who are playing with a garland and, as Vasari says, look as if they are holding on tight to each other so that they don't tumble to the ground. Their spirit is in deliberate contrast to the dramatic scene below. Although the relief was originally gilded, the present gilding dates mostly from 1889.

Crucifix

The story of Brunelleschi's criticism of this work and his demonstration to his friend Donatello of how he felt Christ should, instead, be represented is told on p. 42. Made in pear wood, with moveable arms (so that it could be used in a Deposition scene), this is an early work of around 1412-15. While the numerous earlier Tuscan Crucifixes had idealized or stylized bodies, this is perhaps the first time Christ was represented with strong features and, as Brunelleschi complained, a "peasant's body". It is an extremely powerful work, unfortunately very difficult to see in this dark chapel against a stained glass window. Brunelleschi's *Crucifix* is kept in Santa Maria Novella.

MUSEO DELL'OPERA DI SANTA CROCE

St Louis of Toulouse

Displayed in a cast of its original tabernacle in the refectory of Santa Croce, this is perhaps the least easy work to appreciate of all Donatello's sculptures in Florence. It is a colossal, over life-size, statue in gilded bronze commissioned in the 1420s by the Parte Guelfa for their tabernacle at Orsanmichele, but removed from there when they sold it in the mid 15th century to the Tribunale della Mercanzia. It was later placed high up on the façade of Santa Croce and then in 1860 moved inside the

MUSEO BARDINI

Two reliefs of the
Madonna and Child
(attributed to
Donatello)

The charming high relief of the *Madonna and Child* (above) in polychrome terracotta has often been attributed to Donatello, but is now thought to be an early work by Luca Della Robbia. Displayed in the same room is the *Madonna dei Cordai* a very unusual polychrome work in wood, stucco, and glass, with a background consisting of an extraordinary mosaic of gilded pieces of leather. It is an undocumented work but its refinements were revealed after its restoration in 1985. Since the angels hold instruments used in the manufacture of ropes, it is thought that it was commissioned by an artisans' corporation of rope-makers (*cordai*).

church and since 1903 has been in its present position. It was Donatello's first work in bronze and was cast in eleven parts. The saint is depicted in a traditional manner, looking towards God for divine inspiration, but is also facing left towards the Duomo to bless the traditional procession in his honour which passed Orsanmichele on its way to Piazza della Signoria. The detailed carving of the crozier is particularly remarkable with three bronze statuettes of classical putti bearing shields, although the upper part has been lost. The statue would have appeared even more splendid when it was in its original position and when the enamel decoration of the mitre was still intact.

VIA PIETRAPIANA

Madonna and Child
(attributed to the workshop of Donatello)

This charming relief, with the Child sucking his thumb, is almost certainly by the workshop of Donatello, although in 1985 it was suggested that it might even be by his own hand. It is included here as it is one of very few Donatellian reliefs of the Madonna and Child to have survived in Florence of the many he is known to have carved (some of the most beautiful are now in the museums of Berlin, Vienna, London, Boston, and Paris). The problem of attribution of many of these reliefs is one of the most difficult art historical debates produced by the works of Donatello.

This Madonna is in one of a great many delightful street tabernacles which decorate the streets of Florence. They contain painted or sculpted devotional images and are still an integral part of the life of the city, honoured daily with flowers and candles. Many of them have been beautifully restored since 1991.

LOGGIA DEI LANZI

Head of the marble statue of Faith (attributed)

In the spandrels of the beautiful lofty arches of this famous loggia in Piazza della Signoria seven marble statues of the Virtues, against a blue-enamelled ground, were designed by Agnolo Gaddi in 1384-89. When the head of *Faith* fell to the ground, it is thought that Donatello may have been asked to substitute it. If true, this would be an interesting example of the care with which all Florence's monuments were treated in past centuries, when constant maintenance work was carried out to

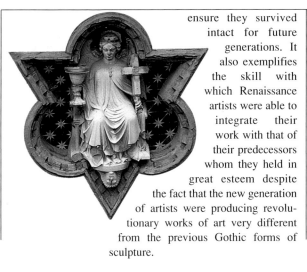

ensure they survived intact for future generations. It also exemplifies the skill with which Renaissance artists were able to integrate their work with that of their predecessors whom they held in great esteem despite the fact that the new generation of artists were producing revolutionary works of art very different from the previous Gothic forms of sculpture.

MUSEO DI SAN MARCO

The convent bell

This bell was commissioned by Cosimo il Vecchio and it has been attributed to Donatello and Michelozzo since its restoration in 1999. It has a frieze of putti and is a fine piece of casting. It was rung here in defence of Girolamo Savonarola, the learned theologian and famous preacher who advocated a return to simple Christian principles, until the prior was arrested in his convent, excommunicated, and imprisoned in Palazzo Vecchio before being burnt at the stake as a heretic and traitor in the piazza outside in 1498. After his death the bell was seized as a symbol of his rebellion against the church, and taken to San Miniato al Monte, but it was returned to the Dominican monks of San Marco in 1511 by order of Pope Julius II.

FONDAZIONE SALVATORE ROMANO (Convent of Santo Spirito)

Two fragments of bas-reliefs of bishop saints (attributed to Donatello)

Since these were found in Padua they have for long thought to have been fragments from the altar made by Donatello in the Basilica of Il Santo in Padua. Although they are very minor works and damaged, and with an uncertain attribution, it is interesting to have a possible testimony in Florence of Donatello's years he spent in Padua working on the most important sculptures he produced outside his native city.

THE DELLA ROBBIA FAMILY

T he idea of glazing terracotta sculpture was due to the sculptor Luca della Robbia in the 1440s and the exceptional quality of the glazing remained a secret in his family for three generations. No other contemporary artist or anyone in succeeding centuries was ever to imitate this technique with the same success. The Della Robbia workshop in Florence was extraordinarily prolific and produced countless works in this new material, including typical blue-and-white Madonnas for private devotion, altarpieces, and coats-of-arms within garlands of fruits and flowers, which were exported all over Europe in the 15th century, and which to this day are to be seen in collections throughout the world. The two most famous components of the family Luca, and his nephew Andrea lived to a very old age (respectively 82 or 83 and 90). Della Robbian works were extremely popular in the late 18th century in England, and they still represent one of the most appealing and delightful aspects of Florentine Renaissance art. As John Pope-Hennessy observed when considering the art of Luca della Robbia "with no great artist of the 15th century is contact easier or more direct".

Giovanni della Robbia, *A Bishop Saint*. Florence, Certosa del Galluzzo

The colourful luminous Della Robbian works are usually blue and white, but sometimes have additional details in green, yellow or mauve. They were produced by adding a layer of enamel to the terracotta sculpture, on which oxides were sometimes applied for colour, and then the work was given a lead glaze. However the exact composition of the preparation of these various layers remained a secret of the Della Robbia workshop.

Luca della Robbia was born in 1399 or 1400, and came from a family who had long been dyers (their surname was derived from a plant found in Tuscany called 'robbia', whose root produces a crimson dye). He began life as a highly skilled and sensitive marble sculptor, possibly training under Nanni di Banco, and, like his contemporaries was greatly influenced by ancient classical sculpture, although we do not know if he ever visited Rome. He certainly knew well and possibly worked with Donatello (13 or 14 years his senior) and Lorenzo Ghiberti and was a friend of Masaccio's, and frequented the circle of Florentine Humanists. However, very little is known about his early activity as a sculptor.

His first important work and his masterpiece was in marble: the famous *cantoria* for the Duomo, a commission he received from the Opera del Duomo, to form a pair with another organ loft which was ordered by them from Donatello. The high reliefs of children, singing, dancing, and playing musical instruments are one of the most pleasing productions of the Renaissance, and demonstrate Luca's extraordinary skill as a sculptor. The Opera del Duomo also commissioned from him five relief panels to complete the sculptural decoration of the Campanile (all these works are now in the Museo dell'Opera del Duomo), and an altar for the Duomo, which, however, was never completed (two panels for it are preserved in the Bargello museum). In 1434 Leon Battista Alberti in his *De Pictura* mentions Luca, along with Brunelleschi, Ghiberti, Masaccio and Donatello as being the five artists responsible for the beginning of Florentine Renaissance art. We have no evidence that Luca ever left Florence throughout his long life.

The reason Luca turned to glazing terracotta sculpture in the early 1440s and abandoned almost totally other materials, has never been satisfactorily explained. But recent studies have suggested that it may well have been due to the influence of his friend Brunelleschi who decided that certain colourful elements would enhance his architectural works. This seems all the more likely when we consider that Luca's two very early works in enamelled terracotta, the lunettes over the sacristy doors in the Duomo, are documented as being ordered by Brunelleschi, specifically in glazed terracotta, to brighten the huge area at the foot of his immense cupola, which had just been completed.

Luca later provided the beautiful blue-and-white tondoes of the twelve *Apostles* in the Cappella dei Pazzi designed by Brunelleschi, and many scholars now believe Brunelleschi himself designed the four polychrome roundels of the *Evangelists* in this chapel (although these are also attributed to Donatello or Luca). Luca's nephew Andrea later filled the tondoes in Brunelleschi's Loggia degli Innocenti.

Giovanni della Robbia and Santi Buglioni, detail from the frieze showing *Works of Mercy*. Pistoia, Ospedale del Ceppo

Luca's other masterpieces in glazed terracotta in Florence include the ceilings of two chapels in San Miniato al Monte, the tomb of Benozzo Federighi in Santa Trinita, and three of the *stemmi* on the outside of Orsanmichele. Although extremely beautiful examples of his numerous famous half-length blue-and-white Madonna reliefs are preserved in the Bargello museum and in the Spedale degli Innocenti, many more can now be seen all over the world, including Paris, Berlin, New York, Oxford, and Copenhagen. They continue a tradition of Florentine Madonnas used as devotional images which were first produced on a large scale by Lorenzo Ghiberti's workshop, and later in the 1430s also by Donatello.

Luca worked for Piero de' Medici in San Miniato, and also decorated his study in Palazzo Medici (although this was destroyed in 1659 and only 12 roundels survive which are now in the Victoria and Albert Museum in London). It is thought that his *Madonna of the Apple* now in the Bargello was owned by the Medici. He also produced an important work in bronze, the doors into the north sacristy in the Duomo.

In 1446, together with his brother Marco, he purchased a house and surrounding land in Via Guelfa, then on the outskirts of the city, and the property was large enough to house a workshop and kiln. However, his brother died just two years later, and Luca was left to look after his six nephews, one of whom, Andrea, became his most famous successor. At the end of Luca's exceptionally successful life, he apparently worked jointly with Andrea on some commissions (such as the two tabernacles in the Collegiata at Impruneta), and the attributions of two very fine female portraits in the Bargello in glazed terracotta are still disputed by art historians between uncle and nephew. Luca was admired by his contemporaries

for his generosity, intellectual qualities and deeply religious spirit.

Andrea (1435-1525) was also extremely skilled and had a highly successful career. Many of his best works are outside Florence in Tuscany, notably at the Franciscan convent of La Verna. But in Florence can be seen his most famous works, the medallions of foundling babies on the colonnade of the Spedale degli Innocenti. Other works by him still in the city include the decoration of the Loggia di San Paolo, as well as lovely tabernacles, altarpieces, and Madonnas (which are usually easy to attribute since he almost always places the Child on the left of the Madonna, whereas Luca almost always chose to put the Child on the right of the Madonna). Andrea was one of 300 Florentines who took a courageous stand in favour of Savonarola against the official Church in 1498, and two of his sons became Dominican monks.

Andrea, who lived to be 90, had numerous children, five of whom worked with him in the Della Robbian workshop in Via Guelfa. Their individual activities have not yet been studied in depth, except for that of his ablest son, Giovanni (1469-1521) who is noted for his particularly colourful and elaborate works, typical examples of which can be seen in the Bargello museum. Giovanni also made a *lavabo* in the sacristy of Santa Maria Novella, a large tabernacle in Via Nazionale, and the 66 very fine roundels in the great cloister in the Certosa del Galluzzo, as well as numerous vases and *stemmi*. Another of Andrea's sons, Girolamo, went to work for Francis I of France in about 1517 and stayed there all his life (he died there in 1566).

The fact that glazed enamelled terracotta is so resilient to the elements makes it particularly suitable for the exterior of buildings, and indeed Tuscany is full of Della Robbian *stemmi* (coats-of-arms or emblems) decorating the exterior of town halls, lunettes over church portals, or Madonnas in tabernacles in streets or country lanes. It is extraordinary that the Della Robbia workshop was able to produce such a huge quantity of instantly recognisable works in the space of some 75 years. But with the death of Andrea's sons, the workshop halted production, and only Benedetto Buglioni (who apparently stole the 'secret' of their technique through a woman who worked for them in Via Guelfa) and his pupil Santi Buglioni went on producing some works of good quality (such as the lunettes over the portals of Ognissanti and the Badia Fiorentina, and part of the Ospedale del Ceppo frieze in Pistoia) at the end of the 15th century before the art practically died out. But its popularity remained such, that in the 19th century extremely successful imitations were made, including four more babies to fill the roundels on an extension to the right and left of the Innocenti portico, which are extremely close in style to the originals beside them, and the *Stemma dei Beccai* on the exterior of Orsanmichele.

Although Florence is still full of Della Robbian works, to appreciate them to the full it is necessary to travel outside the city into Tuscany, where there are many more very fine works, such as Luca's extremely moving *Visitation* group in the church of San Giovanni Fuorcivitas in Pistoia, Andrea's altarpieces in the convent of La Verna and at the Osservanza just outside Siena, and the frieze of the Ospedale del Ceppo in Pistoia by Giovanni.

Luca della Robbia
The bronze doors of the north sacristy

The doors are Luca's only documented work in bronze, begun in 1445. For this commission he formed a partnership with Michelozzo who was particularly skilled in casting bronze. As a young man Luca trained as a goldsmith and possibly worked in the workshop of Lorenzo Ghiberti while Ghiberti was at work on the bronze Baptistery doors.

DUOMO

Luca della Robbia
Two Kneeling Angels

Modelled in white glazed terracotta, these were also commissioned from Luca for this area of the cathedral in 1448, and are his first documented free-standing sculptures in this material. Made to flank the altar, they are holding candlesticks.

Luca della Robbia
Resurrection and *Ascension*

These were Luca's first important works in enamelled terra-cotta, ordered by Brunelleschi who was in charge of the building works of the Duomo in 1442-44, having just completed his extraordinary cupola. They provide a luminous colourful element in this area of the cathedral which is somewhat gloomy and bare. The blue-and-white *Resurrection*, over the door into the north sacristy, is particularly fine, and the original iconographical composition for this familiar subject was copied by later artists. It would have been even more striking in its original state when it had a gilded surface. The influence classical works had on Luca can be recognized in this work.

In the *Ascension* relief the colour green is added to the blue-and-white, for the naturalistic details.

ORATORY OF THE MISERICORDIA

Andrea della Robbia
*Madonna and Child with Saints Cosmas
and Damian*

This was commissioned by Francesco Sassetti from Andrea della Robbia for his chapel in the Badia Fiesolana. Francesco was a merchant, manager of the Medici bank, and a typical figure of his time and so this commission demonstrates the high esteem held for Della Robbian works in Renaissance Florence. Francesco probably chose to include the Medici patron saints in his altarpiece as a tribute to them. An early work, it shows the influence of Luca. It was sold to the Compagnia della Misericordia in 1812, a charitable institution founded in 1244 which still gives free help to those in need, and they put it on the altar of their chapel. It is known that Andrea's uncle Luca was an active member of this lay confraternity, which continues its remarkable work in Florence to this day through some 2000 volunteers.

MUSEO DELL'OPERA DEL DUOMO

Luca della Robbia
Cantoria

Although known since the 18th century as a *cantoria*, or singing gallery, this was made as an organ-loft for the new organ installed in the Duomo in 1438 above one of the sacristy doors. It formed a pair with another similar work commissioned from Donatello at the same time for a restored organ above the opposite sacristy door. This was Luca's first important commission and his masterpiece of marble sculpture. As the inscription indicates, the charming sculptured panels illustrate Psalm 150. The children (some of them drawn from Classical models, such as antique gems, and Roman sarcophagi), dancing, singing, or playing musical instruments, are exquisitely carved within a beautiful architectural framework which

shows the influence of Brunelleschi. Although the details must have been very difficult to see in its original setting in the Duomo, it was greatly admired by his contemporaries and established Luca as the most important sculptor then working in Florence, second only to Donatello, and it was to have a great influence on his successors such as Desiderio da Settignano.

The original panels are now displayed beneath the reconstructed *cantoria*: both this work and that of Donatello were partly dismantled in 1688 and moved in 1839 when the upper parts were altered. The two *cantoria* have been displayed together in this museum since 1889.

Andrea della Robbia
Two lunettes

The enamelled terracotta relief of the *Madonna and Child* by Andrea is displayed in the same room as the flat enamelled lunette of *God the Farther between two Angels*, also attributed to Andrea.

Luca della Robbia
Five reliefs from the Campanile

Philosophy

After the success of Luca's *cantoria*, he received another commission from the Opera del Duomo to supply five reliefs for the lower register of the exterior of the Campanile to complete the early 14th century decoration by Andrea Pisano of Giotto's architectural masterpiece. These originals, unfortunately greatly damaged, were only removed from the north face of the Campanile in 1965. The design of the hexagonal frames and size of the panels follow those of the earlier works, and continue the iconographical scheme which illustrated the Arts and Industries: it is thought that the subjects may have been chosen by the eminent Florentine humanist Leonardo Bruni, who was also a Greek scholar. They probably represent *Grammar*; *Philosophy* or *Dialectic* (the two figures in discussion may represent Plato and Aristotle, and show the influence of Donatello's bronze doors in the Sagrestia Vecchia in San Lorenzo); *Poetry* or *Rhetoric* (represented by Orpheus); *Arithmetic*; and *Astrology* or *Geometry* (with the figure of Pythagoras).

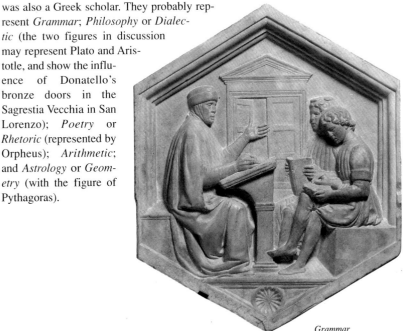

Grammar

ORSANMICHELE

Stemma della Mercanzia

Stemma dei Maestri di Pietra e Legname

Right: *Stemma dei Medici e degli Speziali*

Luca della Robbia
The stemmi on the exterior

The various guilds (or *Arti*) who commissioned statues of their patron saints for the canopied niches on the exterior of this building marked their ownership of the tabernacles by erecting their *stemmi* or emblems in the roundels above them.

Most of these were carried out in fresco and have since almost totally faded, but two of the guilds as well as the Mercanzia, the merchants' court at which guild matters were adjudicated, commissioned their *stemmi* from Luca della Robbia, and they remain here to this day as a vindication of the durability of the technique of glazing used by Luca. This is the earliest known use of enamelled terracotta for *stemmi*, a material later much used all over Tuscany for coats-of-arms.

The *Stemma dei Medici e Speziali* (physicians and apothecaries) shows the Madonna and Child in high relief in a little tabernacle against a charming background imitating a tapestry, flanked by lilies. The circular stone frame shows evident signs of deterioration, whereas the enamelled terracotta remains in almost perfect state, clearly visible, despite its height, from the street below. Here Luca used all the colours available to him: white, blue, green, yellow and purple. The stemma probably dates from around 1460.

The *Stemma della Mercanzia* commissioned in 1463, shows a huge purple fleur-de-lys in relief within a scallop shell surrounded by a beautiful garland of fruit, leaves, and flowers, tied together with a ribbon.

The *Stemma dei Maestri di Pietra e di Legname* (stonemasons and carpenters, the guild to which architects and sculptors belonged) is, instead, flat, decorated in the 1440s by Luca with inlaid glazed terracotta, showing their emblem of an axe, surrounded by the instruments of their trade (a trowel, hammer and chisel, a pair of calipers and a T-square). The inlaid decoration includes exquisite flowers.

Andrea della Robbia

The *Stemma dell'Arte della Seta* (silk-weavers), the guild to which goldsmiths also belonged, with two cupids on either side of a locked door, surrounded by a garland, is attributed to Andrea.

There is a fifth Della Robbian *Stemma* on the exterior of Orsanmichele above the tabernacle of the *Arte dei Beccai* (butchers' guild), which is a very fine imitation made in 1858 by the Ginori firm on a design by Aristodemo Costoli.

SPEDALE DEGLI INNOCENTI

ACCADEMIA DI BELLE ARTI

Andrea della Robbia
Madonna of the Sacred Girdle and Resurrection

These two lunettes by Andrea were made for two altars in the church of Santa Chiara, but they are now beneath the portico of the Accademia. The *Resurrection* is depicted in blue and white, while the *Madonna of the Sacred Girdle, with Saints Francis and Ursula,* has the addition of charming green flowers. They flank a third Della Robbian polychrome lunette of the *Madonna and Child with Saints,* surrounded by a garland and frieze of heads of putti.

Andrea della Robbia
Medallions on the colonnade

These are the most famous works by Andrea, representing the orphan babies who were tended in this foundling hospital, the first institution of its kind in Europe, opened in 1445. The buildings were designed by Brunelleschi in 1419, and this colonnade of nine arches is one of the first masterpieces of Renaissance architecture. Each of the medallions in the spandrels of the arches were filled in 1487 by Andrea with a baby in swaddling-clothes against a bright blue ground. The last bays on the right and left were added in 1842-3 and the four tondoes were filled with excellent copies, almost indistinguishable from the originals. These tondoes, each with the baby in a slightly different attitude, were one of the most popular images of Renaissance Florence in the 19th century.

Luca della Robbia
Madonna and Child

This is one of Luca's most beautiful reliefs of this familiar subject, made in the late 1440s in enamelled terracotta. It is displayed on the first floor in the Pinacoteca.

Andrea della Robbia
Annunciation

A ndrea della Robbia made this lunette for
the portal of the church of the Spedale
degli Innocenti, but it is now in the main
Cloister (Chiostro degli Uomini).

SANTA TRINITA

Luca della Robbia
Tomb of Benozzo Federighi

T his tomb of the bishop of Fiesole who died in 1450 is the
work of Luca (1454-57). It was made for San Pancrazio,
but was moved several times in the 18th and 19th centuries, and
was finally installed here in 1896. The beautiful marble effigy
is surrounded by an exquisite frame of enamelled terracotta mosaic flowers and fruit on a gold ground. This is in fact only the
upper section of the tomb, and obviously not intended to be
seen as displayed here at eye level. However, its lower position
does mean that all the beautiful details can be studied closely.
This is the only example known of a work in marble by Luca
after 1441, since all his other surviving works from that date
onwards are in enamelled terracotta.

SANTA CROCE

Andrea and Giovanni della Robbia
Altarpieces in the Cappella Medici and Cappella Pulci-Berardi

The altarpiece of the *Madonna and Child with Angels* now in the Cappella Medici, was made by Andrea (c 1480) for a church in the Valdarno. The saints were probably added by an assistant in his workshop. The altarpiece in the Cappella Pulci-Berardi at the east end of the church is by Giovanni.

Luca della Robbia
Tondoes in the Cappella dei Pazzi

This chapel is one of Brunelleschi's great architectural masterpieces. The blue-and-white roundels of the twelve seated *Apostles* in the upper part of the walls of the interior are amongst Luca's best works, and show the level of perfect harmony he reached in decorating Brunelleschi's architectural works. They were his first important commission after his work for the Opera del Duomo.

The attribution of the four bright polychrome roundels of the *Evangelists* in the pendentives of the cupola has been much discussed by art historians, some of whom consider them to be the

SANTA MARIA
NOVELLA

Giovanni della Robbia
Lavabo in the sacristy
This is the first
documented work by
Giovanni (1498),
beautifully modelled,
which includes a
charming landscape.

work of Luca, or even Donatello (and glazed by the Della Robbia), while recent scholarship tends to suggest that they were designed by Brunelleschi himself in collaboration with Luca.

The portico of the chapel is thought to have been designed by Giuliano da Maiano, and in the centre of the barrel vault is a very original shallow cupola lined with delightful polychrome enamelled terracotta by Luca, with a garland of fruit surrounding the Pazzi arms in the centre. Over the door is a very beautiful blue-and-white medallion of *St Andrew*, also by Luca (c 1461). The terracotta frieze of cherubs' heads is thought to have been produced by the Della Robbian workshop.

LOGGIA DELL'OSPEDALE DI SAN PAOLO

Andrea della Robbia
Roundels and lunette

This handsome loggia decorates the south-west side of Piazza Santa Maria Novella. The hospital building was reconstructed by Michelozzo for St Antoninus, the Dominican reformer and Archbishop of Florence who died in 1459, but the loggia, a free copy of Brunelleschi's Innocenti colonnade, was only finished in 1489-96. In the spandrels are seven polychrome terracotta roundels of *Franciscan Saints* by Andrea, flanked by two tondoes with a *Poor Man* and a *Rich Man kneeling before Christ*, which may be by his sons Marco and Luca. On the two extreme ends are unusual half tondoes with partly unglazed portrait busts of the master of the hospital, originally painted to show the flesh colour and red cloak, and the date building began (1451) and was completed (1495).

The very fine lunette above the handsome portal at the far end of the arcade represents the *Meeting of St Francis and St Dominic*. This unusual and moving work had a symbolic sig-

nificance since it referred to the possible unification of the two mendicant orders advocated by the two priors of San Marco, St Antoninus and Savonarola. Both the medallions and the lunette are among the least well known Della Robbian works of first importance, and they have recently been beautifully cleaned.

MUSEO NAZIONALE DEL BARGELLO

Works by Luca della Robbia

Exhibited in the great hall on the first floor with the master-pieces of Donatello, the *Madonna of the Rose Garden* and the *Madonna of the Apple* are among Luca's most beautiful enamelled terracotta Madonna reliefs. The *Madonna of the Rose Garden* takes its name from the charming hedge of white thornless roses in the background. *The Madonna of the Apple* (c 1460) formed part of the Medici collection, and is sometimes identified with an enamelled terracotta Madonna known to have

Madonna of the Rose Garden (left); *Madonna of the Apple* (right)

Deliverance of St Peter from Prison (left); *Crucifixion of St Peter* (right)

been kept by Lorenzo il Magnifico in his bedroom. Against a rich blue ground, it preserves its original gilded wood tabernacle. The chubby nude Child clutching an apple leans his head against that of the Madonna, who has a particularly lovely head.

There is discussion among art historians about the *Bust of a Lady* (probably a female Saint), the attribution of which vacillates between Luca and Andrea. The two unfinished marble reliefs of the *Deliverance of St Peter from Prison* and *Crucifixion of St Peter* were commissioned from Luca in 1439 by the Opera del Duomo for an altar in the Duomo, but the project, for some unknown reason, was abandoned. The tondo of the *Madonna and standing nude Child* (with his finger in his mouth) *with two Angels*, enclosed within a garland of yellow and white flowers, although only usually considered to be by Luca's workshop, is particularly fine, and the head of the Madonna is very beautiful. The *Madonna and Child* from Santa Maria Nuova is in its original wood tabernacle. The dark blue ground was originally gilded. The Child, with curly hair, dressed in a tunic, sits in a stiff upright

Madonna and Child from Santa Maria Nuova

Madonna and Child with Angels

Portrait of a Lady

position, holding the Madonna's thumb and little finger. The *Stemma of Amico della Torre* displayed in the loggia is now usually considered an early work by Luca. It shows two winged putti holding the coat-of-arms which includes a tower beneath an elaborate tournament helmet with a bearded head in profile on its crest.

In a room off the chapel which displays goldsmiths' work, the bronze *Dove* by Luca from his Peretola tabernacle (see p. 96) is preserved.

Dove from the Peretola Tabernacle

The circular high relief with the *Portrait of a Lady* displayed in a room on the upper floor which contains works mostly by Andrea, is now considered to be the work of Luca by some scholars.

Stemma of Amico della Torre

Works by Andrea della Robbia

Two works in the Sala del Consiglio Generale showing the *Madonna and Child with two Angels*, one a lunette from Via dell'Agnolo, and the other a tondo, are both now usually considered to be early works of Andrea. The lunette has a garland of white daisies, and two angels holding vases of lilies. Andrea is also very well represented in this museum in a room on the second floor devoted to him and his workshop, in the centre of which is his delightful *Bust of a Boy*. His other works here include two charming tabernacles: the *Madonna of the Cushion*, with delicate decorations on the tabernacle (probably with the collaboration of his son Giovanni) and the exquisite *Madonna of the Stonemasons and Architects* (Maestri di Pietra e Legname), which is his first documented work (1475). The instruments of their trade are shown in the frame, and the figure of the Madonna is particularly lovely and the standing Child, with his finger in his mouth is very appealing. There is a delightful frieze of cherubs' heads and then an outer frame of flowers. Below is a stone relief with two chubby winged cherubs.

There are several versions of an *Adoration of the Child*, attributed to Andrea's workshop, with the elegant kneeling Virgin bending towards the Child who has one of his arms raised towards her, and lilies in the background and two cherubs' heads above. A tondo in blue and white shows the *Madonna and standing Child* encircled with cherubs' heads and seraphim. Also in this room are two rectangular panels of the *Flagellation* and *Ascension* by Andrea, showing the influence of Luca. The delicate circular high relief of a *Female Head* is now usually attributed to Luca. The interesting unglazed terracotta four figure group of the *Lamentation over the Dead Christ* by Andrea, displayed in the room with works mostly by Giovanni, was acquired by the museum in 1998.

Bust of a Boy

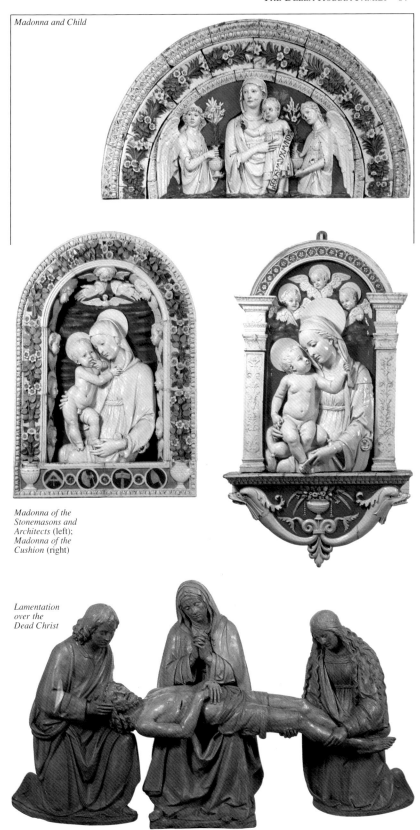

Madonna and Child

Madonna of the
Stonemasons and
Architects (left);
Madonna of the
Cushion (right)

Lamentation
over the
Dead Christ

Works by Giovanni della Robbia

Many of Giovanni's works are exhibited together in one room on the second floor and include a *Bust of Bacchus* and a tondo (partly unglazed) of the *Madonna and Child with the Young St John*, with a pretty, colourful background. The very elaborate altarpiece of the *Nativity* was made for the church of San Girolamo delle Poverine in 1521. Some parts are better than others such as the two kneeling angels at the base of

Bust of Bacchus
Above: *Nativity*

the frame with wooden wings, and the Madonna. Another large altarpiece shows the *Pietà between St John and Mary Magdalen* (1514, from the Ospedale di Santa Maria della Scala), and the statue of *St Dominic* in a niche is particularly striking, with a delicate motif of candelabra. The two lunettes with the *Annunciation* and *Burial of Christ* from Santissima Annunziata are particularly good. The tondo of the *Adoration of the Child with the Young St John* by Luca and Andrea, was given its frame and the angels were added c 1520 by Giovanni. Giovanni also ap-

Pietà between St John and Mary Magdalen
Lunettes showing the *Deposition* (page 88) and the *Annunciation* (below)

St Apollonia;
Francesco Rustici,
Noli Me Tangere (right)

parently glazed the large *Noli Me Tangere* by Francesco Rustici exhibited here. The charming bust of *St Apollonia*, from the church of the same name, is also by Giovanni. There are a number of very colourful reliefs of the same subject by Giovanni's followers, Benedetto and Santi Buglioni, in this room, as well as a particularly fine seated *Madonna and Child* (partly unglazed) by Benedetto.

Stemma of the Bartolini Salimbeni

In a room which displays part of the Medici collection of Italian majolica there is a superb large garland with the *Bartolini-Salimbeni* and *Medici emblems* also by Giovanni. The other tondoes here with *St Francis and St Ursula* also have wonderful garlands of fruits.

SAN MINIATO AL MONTE

Luca della Robbia
Roof and ceiling of the Cappella del Crocifisso

The exquisite little tabernacle in front of the raised choir at the end of the nave was commissioned by Piero il Gottoso de' Medici from Michelozzo in 1448 to house a miraculous Crucifix. Luca provided the enamelled terracotta roof which is decorated with a pattern of scales in the Medici colours of white, mauve and green, and the coffered ceiling which has blue octagons.

Piero also had Luca decorate his study in enamelled terracotta in Palazzo Medici, but it was destroyed, except for the twelve roundels now in the Victoria and Albert Museum in London, in the 17th century.

Luca della Robbia
Ceiling of the Cappella del Cardinale del Portogallo

This funerary chapel of the Portuguese Cardinal James of Lusitania, brother of the Empress of Austria, who died in Florence at the age of 25 incorporates some of the best workmanship of the Florentine Renaissance. It was begun in 1460 by Brunelleschi's pupil Antonio Manetti and contains carving by Antonio Rossellino, a painting by the Pollaiolo (although the original, now in the Uffizi, has been replaced by a copy here), and frescoes by Alesso Baldovinetti. But it was Luca who was chosen to provide its dominant feature, the ceiling, which is one of his masterpieces in enamelled terracotta. Against a background of tiles decorated with classical cubes in yellow, green, and purple, it contains five exquisitely carved medallions representing the *Holy Spirit* (in the form of a dove) surrounded by the four elegant figures of the *Cardinal Virtues*.

Della Robbian works in the apse and sacristy

In the apse of the church there is an enamelled terracotta *Crucifix* made in the Della Robbian workshop, and in the sacristy two Della Robbian *statuettes*.

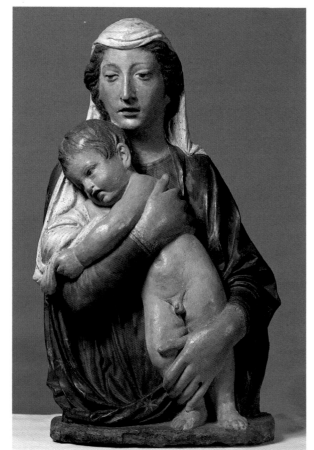

SANTI APOSTOLI

Andrea and Giovanni della Robbia
Tabernacle

At the end of the north aisle, this *Tabernacle for the Sacrament* was made in 1512 by Andrea, and was one of his last works. He was probably helped by assistants from his workshop, and his son Giovanni may have made the putti at the top.

SANTA FELICITA

Luca della Robbia or his workshop
Madonna and Child

This beautiful polychrome terracotta half-length figure of the *Madonna and Child* in the sacristy has been attributed to Luca della Robbia or his workshop since its restoration in 1980.

SAN GAETANO

Andrea della Robbia
Madonna and Child

In the first chapel on the south side of the church this *Madonna* in glazed terracotta was made by Andrea in 1465-70.

STREET TABERNACLES IN FLORENCE

Andrea della Robbia, Tabernacle in Via Sant'Antonino (left); Giovanni della Robbia, Tabernacle in Via dei Macci (right)

The enamelled terracotta *Madonna and Child* at the end of Via Sant'Antonino, placed high up on the corner of Piazza dell'Unità Italiana, is by Andrea. Surrounded by a worn stone tabernacle the Madonna and standing Child against a blue ground are still in very good condition (protected from the pigeons by glass). Very close by, on the corner of Via Sant'Antonino and Via dell'Amorino another Della Robbian tabernacle survives above a popular used clothes stall. It shows the *Madonna in Adoration* above a plaque invoking passers-by to respect the Virgin ("*Rispettate Maria Santissima*").

Andrea's son Giovanni made the lunette in Via della Scala, and the statuette of *St Ambrose* in the little tabernacle high up on the corner of Via dei Macci, just opposite the church of Sant' Ambrogio.

But Giovanni's most impressive street tabernacle is on Via Nazionale, at the end of Via del-l'Ariento. It is called the *Taberna-colo delle Fonticine* since it serves as a monumental fountain (one of the few public drinking fountains left in Florence) and the pavement widens out in front of the seven cherubs' heads from most of which the water still flows. Surrounded by an elaborate pietra serena taberna-cle with a little terracotta roof, and a frame with busts of saints, there is a very fine enamelled terracotta Madonna and Child between Saints James the Greater, Laurence, Bar-bara and Catherine of Alexandria (dated 1522). However the glass in front of it and the traffic in the road make it difficult to examine the tab-ernacle closely.

Giovanni della Robbia, *Tabernacolo delle Fonticine*

**CONVENTO
DELLA MADDALENA**
(Le Caldine)

Andrea della Robbia
and his workshop
Presepio
  This little
Dominican convent is
on the Via Faentina
just beyond the village
of Le Caldine some
way along the
Mugnone valley
below Fiesole. In the
church are life-size
terracotta figures of
the *Madonna and St
Joseph with the Christ
Child* attributed to
Andrea della Robbia
and his workshop,
against a painted
background. The work
is documented in the
convent archives for
the year 1515. Above
is a fresco of the
Annunciation by Fra'
Bartolomeo who lived
here.

DELLA ROBBIAN WORKS IN FIESOLE

I n the Duomo, on the west wall, is a seated statue in yellow and white enamelled terracotta of *St Romulus*, patron saint of Fiesole, dated 1521 and attributed to Giovanni. Above is a medallion with a garland enclosing the coat-of-arms of Bishop Guglielmo de' Folchi who commissioned the statue. The statue and medallion were moved here in 1782 from near Rufina by Bishop Ranieri Mancini, together with another work by Giovanni (a *Madonna Enthroned* with the patron saints of Fiesole) which is now in a chapel in the seminary (not normally open to the public). In the church of Santa Maria Primerana at the upper end of the main piazza of Fiesole is a *Crucifixion with St John and Mary Magdalen* by Andrea. Its provenance is uncertain and it has been moved several times, but it is now in the left transept.

Just out of the piazza is the Museo Bandini which contains no less than 22 Della Robbian works collected by Angelo Maria Bandini born in Fiesole in 1726, the first librarian of the Biblioteca Marucelliana and later of the Biblioteca Laurenziana. Together with his remarkable collection of 13th-15th century Florentine paintings he arranged these in the oratory of Sant' Ansano and left them to the Diocese of Fiesole in 1803. The collection was moved in 1913 to this pretty little building built specially for it by Giuseppe Castellucci. The Della Robbian works on the ground floor have been kept in store for many years, although there are plans to exhibit them again. They are especially noteworthy as examples of the renewed interest in Della Robbian works at the beginning of the 18th century, which continued with even greater emphasis into the 19th century.

Above: Giovanni della
Robbia, *St Romulus*

Andrea della Robbia,
*Crucifixion with
St John and
Mary Magdalen*

SANTA MARIA (Settignano)

Workshop of Andrea della Robbia
Madonna and Child with two Angels

In the sanctuary this beautiful statuary group of the *Madonna and Child with two Angels* in white enamelled terracotta is attributed to the workshop of Andrea della Robbia.

CERTOSA DEL GALLUZZO

Giovanni della Robbia
Tondoes with busts of saints and prophets

The 66 majolica tondoes with busts of saints and prophets which decorate the Great Cloister of this monastery founded in 1342 by the Carthusians (and which since 1958 has been inhabited by a few Cistercian monks) are the most important work of Giovanni (with the possible help of his brother, Luca 'il giovane' or Giovanni Francesco Rustici). Mostly in yellow and white they provide an extremely striking decoration to this beautiful peaceful cloister off which are the monks' cells, each with three rooms, a loggia and a little garden.

Tondoes showing
Saints Lucy and
Agatha and a *Prophet*

SANTA MARIA (Peretola)

Luca della Robbia
Tabernacle from Sant'Egidio

U nfortunately this church is not easy to reach from the centre of Florence, as it is on the north-western outskirts of
the city near the airport. But the tabernacle is of the greatest importance since it is Luca's first documented work in enamelled
terracotta (1441). It was made for the choir of the church of
Sant'Egidio in Florence which had been decorated with frescoes of scenes of the *Life of the Virgin* by Domenico Veneziano
(destroyed in 1594). The tabernacle, in fact probably made as
a reliquary, combines marble sculpture with glazed terracotta:
the very beautiful marble sculptures of two classical angels
and a moving *Pietà* in the lunette (showing the influence of

Masaccio) are framed by decoration in colourful enamelled terracotta. The little bronze door decorated with a *Dove* is preserved in the Bargello museum (see p. 85), and the rectangular bronze door below, roughly inserted into the marble, was probably added later.

SANTA MARIA (Impruneta)

Luca and Andrea della Robbia
Two chapels

Some kilometres outside Florence the large village of Impruneta is in beautiful Tuscan countryside. The clay of the soil has been used for centuries to produce terracotta for which the locality is famous. The kilns here still sell beautiful pottery (including flower pots and floor tiles). At the entrance to the presbytery of the church in the large central piazza are two twin chapels (c 1452) attributed to Michelozzo, with beautiful decoration in enamelled terracotta by Luca and Andrea della Robbia. They were reconstructed and restored after severe bomb damage in 1944. The chapel on the right was built to protect a relic of the True Cross given to the church in 1426. It has an enamelled terracotta ceiling and an exquisite relief of the *Crucifixion with the Virgin and St John* in a tabernacle, flanked by the figures of St John the Baptist and a bishop saint. Beneath is a charming predella of angels in adoration. The chapel on the left protects a miraculous painting of the *Virgin* traditionally attributed to St Luke which was ploughed up by a team of oxen in a field near Impruneta. For centuries it was taken to Florence to help the city in times of trouble. The beautiful ceiling is similar to the one in the other chapel, and the frieze of fruit on the exterior incorporates two reliefs of the *Madonna and Child*. The figures of Saints Luke and Paul flank a tabernacle which contains the image of the Madonna and Child which is usually covered and is only exposed on religious festivals.

FRA ANGELICO

Guido di Piero, born around 1395 near Vicchio in the Mugello north of Florence, took the name of Giovanni when he became a Dominican monk sometime after 1418. At first he lived in the convent of San Domenico di Fiesole (and so became known as Fra Giovanni da Fiesole), but when Cosimo il Vecchio commissioned Michelozzo to enlarge the

Luca Signorelli, *The Sermon of Antichrist*, detail thought to be a portrait of Fra Angelico. Orvieto, Cathedral

buildings of the medieval Silvestrine convent of San Marco for the Dominicans, Fra Giovanni moved down to Florence. While Michelozzo was at work between 1437-52 at San Marco Fra Giovanni was called on to fresco some lunettes in the cloister of St Antonino, the chapter house, and the little monastic cells in the dormitory on the first floor. Because of the deeply religious sentiment in his works he came to be known as 'angelico' and 'beato', or blessed, since he seemed to be divinely inspired.

He was clearly influenced by the art of Lorenzo Ghiberti, Gentile da Fabriano and Masaccio and by the mid 1430s he had become one of the most famous artists at work in Florence. He painted numerous altarpieces for churches in and around Florence, and received an important commission from Cosimo il Vecchio to paint a new high altarpiece for the church of San Marco. The Arte dei Linaioli (guild of flax-workers) ordered him to paint the panels of a large tabernacle, designed by Lorenzo Ghiberti, for their headquarters. He was called to Rome by Pope Eugenius IV around 1445 where he frescoed the Chapel of Nicholas V in the Vatican, and in 1447, with the help of Benozzo Gozzoli, he began to fresco the chapel of San Brizio in the Cathedral of Orvieto. However he completed only two sections of the vault over the altar before he was recalled to Rome, and it was only at the end of the century that Luca Signorelli was commissioned to complete the decoration of this famous chapel. Although Angelico returned to work in Florence, he died in Rome in 1455 and is buried there in Santa Maria sopra Minerva. At his death he was considered the most influential Florentine painter of his time, and it is evident that his art was closely studied by younger painters such as Piero della Francesca and Domenico Veneziano.

His frescoes at San Marco are very well preserved and they were exquisitely restored in the early 1980s. In 1921 it was decided to collect all his panel paintings from churches and convents in Florence and environs and display them in the pilgrims' hospice of the convent, so that San Marco has become a museum devoted to works by Fra Angelico. It provides an extraordinary opportunity to study his frescoes and paintings from all

periods of his working life in this beautiful peaceful setting where he lived and worked. They have a universal appeal since they combine a deeply religious sentiment with a sense of serenity and joy, and seem to encourage meditation. At the same time they have a highly intellectual content, and carefully worked out perspective and numerous complicated compositional elements. Fra Angelico's use of colour is also remarkable and he was a master of the technique of fresco as well as that of panel painting. He was also a superb miniaturist and a choir

book decorated by him for the convent also survives at San Marco.

Works by Angelico outside Florence include a superb painting of the *Annunciation* in the Museo Diocesano at Cortona, and another version of this painting made for the convent of Montecarlo and now in the basilica of Santa Maria delle Grazie in San Giovanni Valdarno. Outside Tuscany, there are paintings by Angelico in Rome and Perugia, and important works by him in museums in Madrid, Paris, Washington, and Munich.

Above: Michelozzo's Library.
Florence, Convent of San Marco

Fra Angelico, *Annunciation*.
Cortona, Museo Diocesano

MUSEO DI SAN MARCO

Nearly all Fra Angelico's works are in the Museo di San Marco. This is one of the most delightful museums in Florence, usually peaceful and not overly crowded, and a place which encourages meditation through the masterpieces collected here of Fra Angelico. In Michelozzo's cloister of Sant'Antonino are five frescoes by Angelico, easy to miss since they are at the four corners of the cloister (and the other lunettes have early 17th century scenes). Close to the entrance, above the two doors into the Pilgrims' Hospice are a very worn fresco of *St Thomas Aquinas*, and *Christ as a Pilgrim welcomed by two Dominicans*. The *Pietà* outside the entrance to the Lavatorium has been restored, but the best fresco in this cloister is *St Dominic at the Foot of the Cross* next to a lunette of *St Peter Martyr* (in the corner opposite the entrance to the museum).

Cloister of
Sant'Antonino

In the Pilgrims' Hospice off this cloister is the remarkable collection of panel paintings by Fra Angelico. Most of them date from the 1430s and are very well preserved. The *St Peter Martyr Triptych* was probably his first work executed before 1429. The *Last Judgement* is also an early work from Santa Maria degli Angeli: its unusual shape is explained by the fact that it decorated the upper part of a ceremonial seat in a church. The dance of the blessed with angels in Paradise is separated from the vivid scenes of the dammed in Hell by a stark representation of the empty tombs of the dead which provides a dramatic focus to the painting.

*St Dominic at the Foot
of the Cross*

Last Judgement

Reliquary-tabernacle
with the *Coronation of
the Virgin*; *San Marco
Altarpiece* (right)

The *San Marco Altarpiece* is one of the few works by Angelico to have been damaged by an abrasive used to clean it in
a restoration many years ago. It is one of his most important
works, showing a new sense of space in the foreground, with a
large Anatolian carpet at the foot of the throne, and a delightful
background of cypresses, cedars, and palm trees. Two of the
panels from its predella are displayed on either side illustrating
the *Burial of Saints Cosmas and Damian*, with a remarkable
perspective, and the *Dream of the Deacon Justinian*,
showing a leg transplant. The other predella panels
are now in Munich, Dublin, and Washington.

*Linaioli
Tabernacle*

The *Linaioli Tabernacle* with the Madonna enthroned surrounded by a frieze
of angels playing musical instruments and
four saints on the shutters is remarkable
also for its unusually large dimension (the
marble frame is by Lorenzo Ghiberti). It
is now unfortunately in rather poor condition. There are also exquisitely painted
tiny works, including reliquary-tabernac-
les from Santa Maria Novella: the *Madonna della Stella*, the *Coronation of the
Virgin*, and, a particularly beautiful work
on a bright gold ground, the *Annunciation*
and *Adoration of the Magi*.

The *Deposition* commissioned by Palla Strozzi for the church of Santa Trinita, c 1435-40 is one of Angelico's most beautiful paintings (the earlier cusps are the work of Lorenzo Monaco). The man in the black hat beneath Christ's right arm may be a portrait of Michelozzo. The other *Deposition* was painted for the Compagnia del Tempio (in the background is the long wall of Jerusalem). The lower part of the painting was damaged by the frequent floods of the river Arno which afflict-ed the oratory where it was kept.

The 35 beautifully painted small panels which served as doors of a cabinet in Santissima Annunziata illustrate *Scenes from the Life of Christ*. They are late works and contain superb

Deposition from Santa Trinita, and details

Deposition from the Compagnia del Tempio

Doors of the Cabinet
from Santissima
Annunziata showing
*Scenes from the Life
of Christ*

narrative details. There are also two more altarpieces of the *Madonna and Child with Saints*: one painted for Bosco ai Frati which is a late work (c 1450), and one painted for the convent of Annalena (which preserves most of its predella).

Also off this cloister is the Chapter House with a large fresco of the *Crucifixion and Saints* by Fra Angelico and assistants. Its effect has been altered since its blue ground has been lost and only the red under-painting survives. This is a mystical representation of the Crucifixion rather than a narrative scene.

Annalena Altarpiece
Above: *Bosco ai Frati
Altarpiece*

Crucifixion with Saints

Stairs lead up to the DORMITORY on the first floor with a huge wooden roof beneath which are 44 small monastic cells with their own vault, each decorated with a fresco by Fra Angelico or an assistant working in his studio (the attribution of some of them is still under discussion). When the frescoes were restored in the 1980s the colour of the original plasterwork was returned to the walls of the cells and corridors. At the head of the staircase is the *Annunciation*, justly one of Angelico's most famous works, set in a delightful loggia looking onto a garden. The cells with the most beautiful frescoes, most of them by Angelico's own hand, are those on the outer wall of the entrance corridor. Each one was painted to encourage the lonely monk to meditation, rather than as a decoration of the cell. The *Noli Me Tangere* is one of the few scenes with some delightful botanical details. The lovely *Annunciation* in the third cell is very different in spirit from the scene at the top of the stairs, with a more severe setting and with the two figures almost sculptural in appearance. The *Transfiguration* and *Mocking of Christ* (in the presence of the Madonna and St Dominic) are two more extremely fine works, and the following cells have frescoes of the *Maries at the sepulchre*, the *Coronation of the Virgin*, the *Pre-*

One of the corridors of the dormitory
Above: *Annunciation*

Annunciation (left);
The Mocking of Christ (right)

Noli Me Tangere and
the cell in the first
corridor where the
fresco is located

sentation in the Temple and the *Madonna and Child with Saints* (probably by an assistant).

In the next corridor the cells have frescoes of *Christ on the Cross* by followers of Fra Angelico, and some medieval fresco fragments from the earlier convent. At the end of the corridor are rooms occupied by Savonarola when he was prior of the convent in 1482-87 and 1490-98. The cells on the inner side of this corridor are by assistants of Fra Angelico, but on the wall outside in the corridor is a *Madonna Enthroned with Saints* attributed to the master himself. The beautiful library by Michelozzo on this floor has just been restored and can also be visited.

GALLERIA DEGLI UFFIZI

Coronation of the Virgin

Displayed in room 7 of the Uffizi, this *Coronation of the Virgin* was painted for the church of Sant' Egidio and has a profuse use of gold. The sense of perspective is increased by the arrangement of the little clouds and the angels' crossed trumpets. Also here is a *Madonna and Child* by Angelico, probably the central panel of a polyptich.

ORATORY OF SAN NICCOLÒ AL CEPPO

Crucifixion

In the Oratory of San Niccolò al Ceppo in Via Pandolfini near Santa Croce there is a painting by Fra Angelico of the *Crucifixion with Saints Nicholas of Bari and Francis.* Although this has recently been restored it is hardly ever visible since the oratory is only open when used for concerts.

SAN DOMENICO (Fiesole)

Madonna with Angels and Saints
Madonna and Child

In the church of San Domenico di Fiesole is an altarpiece of the *Madonna with Angels and Saints* painted around 1430 by Angelico for the high altar of the church (but now in the first chapel on the left). The architectural background was added by Lorenzo di Credi in 1501, when the frame was redesigned (the paintings of Saints are by a follower of Lorenzo Monaco). The panels of the predella are copies; the originals are in the National Gallery, London. In the little chapter house of the convent (not usually open to visitors, but ring at No. 4 on the right of the church) there is a beautiful fresco of the *Crucifixion* by Angelico and a detached fresco (with its sinopia) of the *Madonna and Child* also attributed to him.

SANDRO BOTTICELLI

B otticelli, born c. 1445, was one of the greatest and most original painters of the Italian Renaissance, but he fell into oblivion soon after his death and was only 'rediscovered' at the beginning of the 20th century. Today his works in Florence are perhaps the most famous paintings in the city. His real name was Sandro Filipepi, and it is uncertain how he came to be called 'Botticelli', but the word is probably connected with '*battigello*', meaning silversmith (as a boy Botticelli was apprenticed to a goldsmith).

As a young man he spent a number of years in Filippo Lippi's workshop, and some of his early Madonnas clearly show the influence of his master (one of these, now in the Spedale degli Innocenti, is actually a copy of a work by Lippi). It is thought that Botticelli also frequented Verrocchio's studio. One of his earliest public commissions was from the Arte della Mercanzia, who in 1470 ordered a painting of *Fortitude* from him, one of a series of the seven Virtues (the others were produced by Piero del Pollaiolo).

He soon came to the attention of the Medici, and some of his most important works were carried out for Lorenzo il Magnifico's cousin Lorenzo di Pierfrancesco de' Medici including the *Primavera*, and *Pallas and the Centaur*

Sandro Botticelli, *Adoration of the Magi*, detail showing his self-portrait. Florence, Galleria degli Uffizi

which were hung in the Medici palace in Via Larga (the present Via Cavour). They were later moved, together with the *Birth of Venus* to the Medici villa of Castello. His famous *Adoration of the Magi* now in the Uffizi (one of four paintings of the same subject by him), painted for a banker friend of the Medici, includes numerous portraits of the Medici, and the combination in this work of a religious subject with portraits of famous men astounded his contemporaries. This beautiful painting, seen as a homage to the great family, includes Botticelli's own self-portrait.

Apart from his numerous charming Madonnas, many of them tondoes, he also produced some superb altarpieces for churches in Florence (some of them now in the Uffizi). Only a few portraits by him survive in his native city, but they include the remarkable *Portrait of a Man holding a Medal of Cosimo il Vecchio*. This is now thought possibly to be a portrait of Botticelli's brother Antonio who is known to have coined medals for the Medici, since a certain family likeness can be discerned, when compared with Botticelli's self-portrait in his *Adoration of the Magi*, and Filippino Lippi's supposed portrait of him in the frescoes in the Brancacci chapel.

Botticelli was greatly admired in his lifetime, and in 1481 was called to Rome

Sandro Botticelli, drawings showing *Pallas* and the *Angel of the Annunciation*. Florence, Gabinetto dei Disegni e delle Stampe degli Uffizi

by Pope Sixtus IV to work in the Sistine Chapel, together with Cosimo Rosselli, Domenico Ghirlandaio, and Perugino. It seems that Botticelli was particularly highly considered since he was asked to fresco three works there as well as the entire series of portraits of the Popes. In Florence he was also asked to take part in the committee set up in 1504 to decide where Michelangelo's statue of *David* should be placed (together with Giuliano da Sangallo and Cosimo Rosselli he favoured the steps of the Duomo).

He also received commissions from the Vespucci family who were merchants involved in the manufacture of silk who held political office in the 15th century as supporters of the Medici (Amerigo Vespucci, a Medici agent in Seville, five years younger than Botticelli, gave his name to America having made two voyages in 1499 and 1501-02 following the route charted by his Italian contemporary Columbus). The Vespucci were neighbours of the Filipepi in Florence (and it was probably through them that Botticelli was able to enter Lippi's workshop). Their church was Ognissanti, where both families had their tombs, and Botticelli's fresco there of *St Augustine* (a subject of

a number of paintings by him) was paid for by the Vespucci in 1480.

Botticelli was greatly influenced by the neoplatonic philosophical culture which he acquired from the Humanists at the Medici court. This classical background enabled him to produce such remarkable pictures as the *Primavera*, the *Birth of Venus*, and *Calumny*. Scholars still discuss the precise significance of these works, which are extraordinary illustrations of classical myths as well as almost mystical expressions of personal melancholy.

Botticelli was extremely skilled as a draftsman, and accentuated the linear elements in his paintings. His use of colour was superb, often highlighted in gold. His rendering of the nude body was masterly, as can be seen in the *Birth of Venus* and the *Finding of the Body of Holofernes in his Tent*. The botanical details in many of his paintings are also of the greatest interest, and in particular in his *Primavera*. Lorenzo di Pierfrancesco de' Medici commissioned him to illustrate Dante's *Divina Commedia*, and 91 of his beautiful drawings survive (in Berlin and the Vatican; exhibited together for the first time in Rome in 2000).

From 1472 he had a thriving workshop, with at least four assistants, as well as Filippo Lippi's son Filippino, his most intelligent and famous pupil. Towards the end of his life, from 1487 until his death in 1510, he was influenced by the preaching of Savonarola, and some of his last works such as his *Annunciation* and *Coronation of the Virgin*, both now in the Uffizi, illustrate a deeply religious sentiment. Some of his paintings of pagan subjects he apparently destroyed under the influence of the Dominican prior who denounced "immoral luxuries" in his daily sermons and had bonfires lit in Piazza della Signoria to destroy works of art and books.

Although Vasari praises a number of his works which he describes in detail, he makes some rather disparaging remarks about his later life, and after Botticelli's death his works seem to have had remarkably little influence on his contemporaries at a time when Florentine art was dominated by the figures of Leonardo da Vinci and Michelangelo. For centuries he remained practically unknown, and it was only at the beginning of the 20th century, largely through English-speaking art historians such as Bernard Berenson and Herbert Percy Horne, that his remarkable qualities as a painter were recognised, and his works were carefully studied. The Uffizi now owns 21 paintings by Botticelli, although most of them joined the collection only in the late 18th century, the 19th century or the early years of the 20th century. His corpus still contains a great number of works whose attribution is contested.

Florentine painter of the late 15th or early 16th century, *The Martyrdom of Savonarola in Piazza della Signoria*. Florence, Museo di San Marco

GALLERIA DEGLI UFFIZI

Annunciation

Detached in 1920 from the church of San Martino alla Scala, this charming fresco has been displayed on the ground floor of the Uffizi for some years but it is usually very difficult to see. The delightful intimate scene includes the Madonna's bed with white hangings and bedspread, a little Renaissance garden, and floor tiles in perfect perspective. Dated 1481, it is quite different in spirit to Botticelli's later painting of the *Annunciation* exhibited in the main room of his works on the floor above.

Judith returning from the Camp of Holofernes and The Discovery of the Decapitated Holofernes in his Tent

These two exquisite small works (31x24 cm), displayed in room 9, were formerly united as a diptych in a frame (lost at the end of the 18th century) and first documented in the 1580s as a present from Rodolfo Sirigatti to Bianca Cappello. It then passed to her son Don Antonio de' Medici and since 1632 has been carefully preserved in the Uffizi. An early work, the influence of Verrocchio, Pollaiolo and Mantegna can all be seen here. The nude figure of Holofernes is particularly remarkable.

Fortitude

This is Botticelli's first dated work cited in the documents of the time. It was commissioned by the Tribunale della Mercanzia in 1470 and the remarkably elegant figure is clothed in heavy silks as well as armour. It is one of a series of the *Virtues* which decorated the headquarters of the merchants' court in Piazza della Signoria (the other six were painted by Piero del Pollaiolo), and they remained there until 1717.

Primavera

This is one of Botticelli's most important and largest works (203x314 cm), and perhaps now the most famous painting in Florence. It is displayed in the large hall devoted to works by Botticelli in the Uffizi. It was executed probably around 1481 for Lorenzo di Pierfrancesco de' Medici, Lorenzo il Magnifico's younger cousin. For years kept at the Medici Villa di Castello it was moved to the Uffizi in 1815, then transferred to the Accademia, but returned here in 1919. An allegory of Spring, it is thought to have been inspired by a work of Poliziano and by neoplatonic ideals, although its precise significance is still discussed. Set in the Garden of Hesperides of classical myth, in a meadow of flowers within a dark orange grove, there is a rhythmical contact between the figures. To the right Zephyr chases Flora and transforms her into Spring, who is shown bedecked with flowers. In the centre stands Venus with Cupid above her, and beyond the beautiful group of the Three Graces united in dance, is the figure of Mercury (perhaps an idealized portrait of Lorenzo il Magnifico). It is possible that Botticelli took inspiration for the figure of Flora from the Hellenistic Roman sculpture of a *Dancing Girl* (known as *Pomona*) in the Medici collection of ancient sculpture.

The work is richly painted in tempera (with the addition of oil) on poplar wood. The varnishes which had been added in various restorations were removed in 1982 and the painting cleaned so that the original tones were restored to the surface. The botanical details which were revealed after its cleaning include a great variety of spring flowers, most of them still to be found in Lorenzo di Pierfrancesco's Villa di Castello.

Hellenistic Roman sculpture, *Dancing Girl* known as *Pomona*. Florence, Galleria degli Uffizi

*Madonna
of the Loggia*

The attribution of
this work has been
contested for many
years, but it is now
usually considered to
be by Botticelli's own
hand, although the
landscape has been
repainted. It is an
early work, probably
dating from around
1467.

Birth of Venus

This is another of Botticelli's most famous works. It was
probably painted around 1483 for Lorenzo di Pierfrancesco
de' Medici and hung, together with the *Primavera,* in his Villa
di Castello. The pagan subject is taken from a poem by
Poliziano and illustrates the two winds Zephyr and Aura (formerly thought to be the nymph Chloris) blowing Venus ashore
while a female figure identified as Hora or one of the three
Graces, her fluttering dress decorated with cornflowers and
daisies, hurries to cover her nakedness. The elegant figures with
flowing hair, are painted with a remarkable lightness of touch
on canvas, in a decorative linear design. Some of the naturalistic details are highlighted in gold. The classical nude figure of
Venus balances on the edge of a beautiful scallop shell as it
floats ashore. A strong wind blows through this harmonious
Graeco-Roman world.

Madonna of the Magnificat

This beautiful tondo was painted around
1481 and is one of Botticelli's most famous
paintings of the Madonna and Child (there
are replicas in the Louvre and the Pier-
pont Morgan Library in New York).
The very refined composition suggests the figures are projected on a
convex mirror, with a circular
window in the background. It
was sold to the Uffizi in the late
18th century.

Madonna of the Rose Garden

This is one of the earliest of Botticelli's beautiful paintings of the Madonna and Child (c 1470) which still shows the influence of his master Filippo Lippi and of Verrocchio.

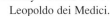

Madonna of the Pomegranate

The composition of this tondo differs from that of the slightly earlier *Madonna of the Magnificat* in that it seems to be reflected in a concave, rather than a convex, mirror. It preserves its beautiful original frame decorated with gilded lilies on a blue ground which suggests it was destined for an office in Palazzo Vecchio. The Child holds an exquisitely painted pomegranate, symbol of the Passion of Christ, and the angels have symbols which allude to the purity and grace of the Virgin (roses and lilies). The melancholy face of the Madonna recalls that of Venus in the *Birth of Venus*. The painting is first documented in the 17th century when it was owned by Cardinal Leopoldo dei Medici.

Coronation of the Virgin and Saints (*San Marco Altarpiece*)

This is one of the earliest altarpieces known where the composition is divided in two: the scene of the *Coronation of the Virgin* in a golden Paradise in the sky above is separated from the four *Saints* on earth below by a delightful group of dancing angels with joined hands. The saints are St John the Evangelist, who indicates the scene above, St Augustine, St Jerome, and St Eligius, patron of the goldsmiths for whose this chapel was painted in San Marco.

The predella includes five scenes related to the Virgin (*Annunciation*) and each of the four Saints (St Eligius is shown in a smithy shoeing a horse). Numerous later 16th century altarpieces, including some fundamental works by Raphael and Titian were to follow this compositional scheme. It is a late work, dating from around 1489, and is one of Botticelli's most profoundly religious paintings. It was in very poor condition probably due to a mistaken preparation of the panel and was then damaged by numerous drastic and unsuccessful restorations. However its quality can now again be appreciated since its careful restoration in 1991.

Madonna and six Saints
(Sant'Ambrogio Altarpiece)

This is the first altarpiece known to have been painted by Botticelli and it has recently been beautifully restored. The two kneeling figures of the Medici saints Cosmas and Damian, once thought perhaps to be Medici portraits, may instead represent the donors. The Madonna is seated on a throne in a refined architectural setting, and the figure of Mary Magdalen on the left is particularly striking.

Madonna and Child in Glory

Dating from around 1470 this charming full-length Madonna includes a glory of seraphim in golden rays. The frame is probably original.

Madonna and Child with six Saints
(San Barnaba Altarpiece)

This is another large altarpiece by Botticelli, showing the Madonna and Child with Saints Catherine of Alexandria, Augustine, Barnabus, John the Baptist, Ignatius, and Michael Archangel, and four angels. It was probably painted around 1487, but it has been partly altered over the centuries and the colours have deteriorated through the addition of varnishes.

Only four of the original seven panels of the predella (see pictures on the left) have survived showing intimate and delicately painted scenes of the *Vision of St Augustine*, the *Pietà*, *Salome with the Head of St John the Baptist*, and the *Extraction of the Heart of St Ignatius*.

Annunciation

One of Botticelli's most beautiful late paintings, there is an extraordinary spiritual bond between the Virgin and the Angel of the Annunciation and the picture is pervaded with a deeply religious sentiment. Vasari records that the work was painted for the monks of Cestello who had their convent in Bor-

go Pinti (later dedicated to Santa Maria Maddalena dei Pazzi) having been commissioned by Benedetto Guardi del Cane, whose coat-of-arms can be seen on the lower part of the original frame. It then found its way to a chapel near Fiesole where it was only re-identified in 1872 and moved to the Uffizi. The composition was probably influenced by Donatello's *Cavalcanti Annunciation* in Santa Croce, and also possibly Filippo Lippi's *Annunciation* in San Lorenzo. The exquisite details include a luminous landscape, and the transparent veils of the two figures.

Adoration of the Magi

This is one of Botticelli's most important paintings, much praised by his contemporaries. In a remarkable setting with a tumble-down stable devoid of animals, and a ruined classical portico, the Madonna and Child with St Joseph seem to take second place to the crowd of worshippers, many of whom are diverted from the Holy scene since they are deep in discussion amongst themselves. Vasari describes the picture in detail and points out that some of the figures are portraits of the Medici. Although their identification is still not certain, scholars tend to agree that the kneeling King at the foot of the Virgin is Cosimo il Vecchio, the second King in a red cloak kneeling in the foreground is Cosimo's eldest son Piero il Gottoso, and the third King on the right is probably Giovanni, Cosimo's other son. The striking figure of a young man beside his horse on the extreme left of the picture is usually identified as Lorenzo il Magnifico. He stands next to Poliziano and Pico della Mirandola. The dark man dressed in black in profile in the group to the right may be Giuliano de' Medici (although it has also been suggested that, instead, this figure represents Lorenzo il Magnifico). Above him, just to the left, the old man with grey hair looking out of the picture is sometimes taken to be a portrait of the donor Gaspare Lami, a banker friend of the Medici, who commissioned the picture for his chapel in Santa Maria Novella. The impressive standing figure in a yellow cloak, also looking at the spectator, is universally accepted as Botticelli's self-portrait.

The painting later came into the possession of the Medici, but its whereabouts is unknown from the early 17th century until 1849 when, attributed to Domenico Ghirlandaio, it joined the Uffizi collection. The composition is remarkable as well as the

Adoration of the Magi (unfinished)

This painting has been kept in the deposits of the Uffizi since it was acquired in 1779 because of its poor condition and is still not regularly exhibited. The last of four paintings Botticelli made of this subject, it was left unfinished by him at his death and it is thought parts of it may be by his workshop. The extraordinary landscape is reminiscent of the work of Leonardo da Vinci.

glowing colours, the naturalistic details, the exquisitely painted peacock, and the vivid portraits. The work is a tribute to the Medici and a recognition of their importance in Florence. Two other earlier paintings of the same subject are now in the National Gallery in London, and a fourth, left unfinished, belongs to the Uffizi (see picture on the left).

Portrait of a Man holding a Medal of Cosimo il Vecchio

R ecently beautifully restored this is one of the best portraits by Botticelli left in Florence. The unusual pose, with the hands foreshortened as they present the spectator with a gold medal inscribed with the profile of Cosimo il Vecchio, is particularly striking. It is known that the medal was coined in 1465 to celebrate Cosimo's title of 'Pater Patriae'. The identification of the sitter has been much discussed, but the most recent hypothesis is that it could be a portrait of Botticelli's brother, Antonio, who was a medallist. The picture was left to the Uffizi by Cardinal Carlo de' Medici in 1666. The typical luminous landscape in the background, with a river, shows the influence of contemporary Flemish paintings.

Calumny

Although relatively small in dimension, this is an extremely complex painting which has generated a great deal of scholarly discussion about its subject matter. It is a late work in which Botticelli combines numerous classical references with a pronounced religious fervour. The theatrical poses of the figures are taken to an extreme limit, and the elaborate painting evidently demands an acute intellectual interpretation. Botticelli was almost certainly influenced by the account in Alberti's treatise on painting of the Greek writer Lucian's description in the 2nd century AD of a picture by the great Greek painter Apelles of the same subject. It shows Botticelli's fascination with classical myths, and the setting is full of classical sculptures and bas-reliefs. On the left is the nude figure of Truth (based on classical sculptures of Venus) next to an old woman in a black cloak representing Penitence. The nude man with his hands joined in prayer, the subject of a calumnious attack, is being dragged by Calumny holding a lighted torch before the enthroned King Midas who is shown beset on each side by allegorical figures representing Suspicion (on his left) and Ignorance (on his right).

The painting was commissioned by Antonio Segni, a Florentine banker who was also a friend of Leonardo da Vinci, and it was then owned by the Medici until at least 1704.

Pallas and the Centaur

This painting was probably intended as a moral or political allegory, the significance of which has been much discussed. It is usually thought that Pallas represents Florence or Lorenzo il Magnifico, and the centaur, half man and half beast represents disorder and barbarism. Pallas, whose clothes are decorated with Lorenzo's emblem and olive branches, is shown taming the centaur, derived from Hellenistic models. It was painted for Lorenzo di Pierfrancesco de' Medici around 1482 and remained in the Medici palace in Florence from 1498 for at least a hundred years. After 1638 it is documented as being in the Villa di Castello together with the *Primavera* and *Birth of Venus*.

SPEDALE DEGLI INNOCENTI

Madonna and Child with an Angel

A very early work, this is a copy from a Madonna by Botticelli's master Filippo Lippi, and probably painted in his workshop in 1465. Unfortunately it has been damaged by excessive cleaning and repainting.

St Augustine

A tiny painting, this succeeds in conveying a sense of monumentality in the figure of the saint in a monochrome barrel-vaulted niche with tondoes enclosing classical profile heads and a lunette with a bas-relief of the Madonna and Child. The exquisitely painted details include a half-drawn curtain, and scraps of paper at the saint's feet with his discarded notes and used quills. The saint is dressed partly as a hermit and therefore it is believed the painting was made as a devotional image for the prior of the Augustinian monks at the convent of Santo Spirito. Vasari mentions it (but with an attribution to Filippo Lippi) in the house of Bernardo Vecchietti, and it is next documented in the 18th century as the property of the English painter Ignazio Hugford, and it was sold to the Uffizi in 1779. It is a late work dated around 1495 and is one of a number of pictures of St Augustine by Botticelli.

GALLERIA PALATINA

Portrait of a Man

The attribution of this engaging portrait of a man in a typical Florentine head-dress was for long contested, but in the 20th century it was recognized by most scholars as an autograph work, even though it has been damaged in the past and partly repainted. It is dated around 1470.

Portrait of a Lady ('La Bella Simonetta')

This portrait is now often attributed to Botticelli's workshop, but it is still a remarkable and extremely unusual work in muted shades of brown, restored in 1989. The pensive young girl in typical Florentine dress is shown in profile and she has never been conclusively identified. The detail of her hair in slight disarray is typical of the skill of Botticelli.

Madonna and Child with the Young St John

The attribution of this work painted on canvas is also uncertain and its provenance is unknown. But since its restoration in 1976 many scholars believe it to be a late work by Botticelli's own hand. The composition is extremely unusual, with the Christ Child almost falling out of his mother's arms to embrace the young boy (St John) who is standing beside her. In the background is a charming rose bush.

GALLERIA DELL'ACCADEMIA

Madonna and Child with the Young St John and two Angels

This is a very beautiful early work showing the influence of Filippo Lippi and Verrocchio, painted for the Ospedale of Santa Maria Nuova around 1468. Unfortunately it is not in good condition and was partly repainted in the 17th century (another, probably earlier version, of the same painting exists in Avignon in France).

Virgin of the Sea

This is a delightful small work not always attributed to Botticelli's own hand. Its name comes from the background, which is typical of numerous works by Botticelli with river scenes or seascapes with boats. Usually dated around 1480 some scholars believe it could be the work of his pupil Filippino Lippi. The delicate features of the exceptionally young Madonna are particularly refined.

OGNISSANTI

GALLERIA CORSINI

**Madonna and Child
with six Angels**

   This tondo is
usually attributed to
Botticelli's workshop,
perhaps on a cartoon
by the master. The
Corsini family
archives document the
acquisition of the
picture in the 17th
century from the Villa
Medici di Careggi. It
is kept in the Galleria
Corsini on Lungarno
Corsini, which was
formed in the 17th
century and survives
as the most important
private collection of
paintings in Florence.

St Augustine

S t Augustine is shown deep in thought in his study with a
clock, an armillary sphere, and a white checked cloth on his
desk. The books are arranged on the shelves flat rather than on
end, and one of them is open at a page with geometrical figures
derived from Euclid. The fresco was commissioned in 1480 by
the Vespucci family whose crest is in the upper part of the fresco and who were neighbours and friends of Botticelli's family,
the Filipepi.

   As a pendant to Domenico Ghirlandaio's *St Jerome*, now on
the wall opposite, it originally decorated the choir screen of the
church. When this was dismantled in the 16th century, the two
frescoes were carefully detached (probably one of the first in-
stances of this practice which became very normal in the 20th
century), and they have both survived remarkably well. Botticelli was evidently fascinated by the figure of St Augustine as a
philosopher and father of the Church since he painted him a
number of times. Here he demonstrates his skill as a fresco
painter, influenced by the fresco techniques of Andrea del
Castagno.

SANTA MARIA NOVELLA

Nativity

Now on the west wall of the church this lunette fresco was first attributed by Bernard Berenson to Botticelli. It was probably formerly in the Lami chapel, for which his famous *Adoration of the Magi* now in the Uffizi was also painted. It was modified and repainted in the 19th century and restored in 1984.

SAN FELICE IN PIAZZA

Triptych of St Roch, St Anthony Abbot and St Catherine of Alexandria (follower of Botticelli)

This is an interesting work very close to Botticelli's style, but probably by a follower, possibly Filippino Lippi. It was painted for another altar of the church, but is now on the north wall near the entrance.

ORATORIO DEL VANNELLA (Corbignano)

Madonna and Child Enthroned

This fresco was first attributed to Botticelli as a very early work by Bernard Berenson who lived nearby at Villa I Tatti. It is a devotional image which for centuries was venerated by the stonemasons and sculptors of Settignano. It is in a charming little country chapel in a beautiful setting. Many scholars are doubtful about its attribution, since it has been frequently repainted.

VILLA LA QUIETE (convento delle Montalve)

Coronation of the Virgin with Saints

This altarpiece in a lovely convent on the outskirts of Florence near the Villa Medici di Careggi is usually attributed to Botticelli's workshop.

DOMENICO GHIRLANDAIO

Ghirlandaio (Domenico di Tommaso Bigordi), born in 1449, was especially skilled as a fresco painter, and he produced some very fine fresco cycles in Florence, the most famous of which is in the huge main chapel in the sanctuary of Santa Maria Novella. He set religious stories against a background of contemporary Florence, thus creating a remarkable picture of his times, when the city was at the height of its glory under the leadership of Lorenzo il Magnifico, the famous Medici ruler and humanist scholar, born in the same year as Ghirlandaio (and who died just two years before him). In many of the scenes of his fresco cycles Ghirlandaio introduced portraits of his rich cultivated contemporaries (only some of whom, however, can now be identified with certainty).

Domenico Ghirlandaio, *Miracle of the Boy brought back to Life*, detail showing his self-portrait. Florence, Santa Trinita

Ghirlandaio was greatly influenced by classical Rome which he visited several times, and he included numerous buildings in his paintings and frescoes which are derived from ancient Roman edifices, together with decorative details often imitating classical marble reliefs. It is probable that Alesso Baldovinetti was Ghirlandaio's master. His use of remarkably vivid colours can be seen in the altarpieces he painted for churches in the city, where his debt to contemporary Flemish

painting can also be discerned. He was clearly influenced by the huge triptych of the *Adoration of the Shepherds*, commissioned by the Medici agent in Bruges, Tommaso Portinari from Hugo van der Goes, and shipped back to Florence in 1475 for his family chapel in Sant'Egidio (now displayed in the Uffizi). As his fame increased he set up a workshop to assist him in his work, which included his brother Davide and Sebastiano Mainardi, who later became his brother-in-law. Although the overall schemes of his fresco cycles must have been planned by him, and he probably carried out most of the cartoons, it is sometimes hard to detect in the frescoes themselves just where he himself painted and where his assistants were set to work. We know that he was greatly admired in his lifetime and was called to Rome by Sixtus IV to work in the Vatican library and the Sistine chapel, and he also frescoed the Cappella di Santa Fina in the Collegiata of San Gimignano. Since Ghirlandaio was one of the most important painters of his time, Michelangelo, while still a boy, joined his workshop in 1488 while Domenico was at work on completing the Santa Maria Novella frescoes. Ghirlandaio was technically very able, and, indeed most of his frescoes and paintings are extremely well preserved. Vasari records Ghirlandaio's enthusiasm as a fresco painter and quotes him as saying "ora che io ho comminciato a conoscere il modo di quest'arte, mi duole che non mi sia allogato a dipignere a storie il circuito di tutte le mura della città di Fiorenza" [now that I have begun to understand the technique of this art, I am sad that I haven't been assigned to paint stories on the entire circle of walls around the city of Florence]. He also de-signed stained glass windows (notably the beautiful window at the east end of Santa Maria Novella) and mosaics (including the lunette over the Porta della Mandorla of the Duomo). He married twice and had nine children in all, one of whom Ridolfo also became a well-known painter. In 1494 Ghirlandaio died of the plague, when still a young man, and he was buried in Santa Maria Novella.

SANTA MARIA NOVELLA

Main Chapel

His most famous fresco cycle is in the Gothic sanctuary of Santa Maria Novella, commissioned from him in 1485 by Giovanni Tornabuoni, who was for years manager of the Rome branch of the Medici bank and whose sister Lucrezia married

Piero il Gottoso. The contract for the work survives with detailed specifications about the subjects required and imposing a time limit of four years for the completion of the work. They are extremely extensive, with no less than seven scenes on all three walls, including a very large *Coronation of the Virgin* in the lunette above the huge window. Although the overall scheme belongs to Domenico, his assistants also worked here with him, including Sebastiano Mainardi, and it is now in some places very difficult to distinguish between their different hands.

From the crossing of the church the altar hampers the view of the lowest registers which have the most important scenes of the cycle, but visitors can now enter the sanctuary every hour to examine the frescoes. They replaced a fresco cycle by Orcagna which formerly decorated this Gothic chapel (fragments of which were found and detached from the vault and they are now displayed in a room off the cloister). Ghirlandaio's frescoes illustrate the *Lives of the Virgin* (on the left wall) *and St John the Baptist* (on the right wall), and include numerous portraits of members of the Tornabuoni family. On the end wall, above the window, is a large *Coronation of the Virgin*, and below are scenes of the *Miracle of St Dominic, Death of St Peter Martyr, Annunciation, St John the Baptist in the Desert*, and (in the lowest register) the two kneeling figures of the donors, *Giovanni Tornabuoni and his Wife Francesca Pitti* (a posthumous portrait). In the vault are the four *Evangelists*. The beautiful stained glass window (c 1491) was also designed by Ghirlandaio.

The scenes on the left wall illustrate the *Life of the Virgin*. On the lowest register is the *Expulsion of St Joachim from the Temple* which includes, in the group on the right, Domenico's self portrait, and portraits of his brother Davide, Sebastiano Mainardi and (probably) Alesso Baldovinetti, with whom Domenico studied as a young man. The portico in the background seems to be derived from the Loggia dell'Ospedale di San Paolo which can still be seen (recently restored) opposite the façade of the church in Piazza Santa Maria Novella. The adjoining beautiful scene of the *Birth of the Virgin* generally considered to be entirely by the hand of Ghirlandaio himself, is signed in the panelling to the right of the standing girl dressed

Expulsion of St Joachim from the Temple, and detail showing the presumed portraits of Domenico Ghirlandaio and his brother Davide

Presentation in the Temple
Above: *Birth of the Virgin*

in white and gold (usually identified as Ludovica Tornabuoni, Giovanni's daughter). The graceful girl in the act of pouring water into a basin is a charming detail. The meeting of Anna and Joachim is also incorporated into this scene: the couple are shown tenderly embracing at the top of the stairs. The striking frieze of putti skillfully imitates a sculptured relief.

On the register above, the *Presentation in the Temple* includes a very fine figure of a man sitting on the steps, but the collaboration of both Davide Ghirlandaio and Sebastiano Mainardi can be detected in this panel. The scene beside it shows the *Marriage of the Virgin*. The remaining scenes on the upper part of the wall illustrate the *Adoration of the Magi* (the only fresco here damaged from humidity), the *Massacre of the Innocents* (thought to have been painted mostly by Davide Ghirlandaio), and, in the lunette at the top of the wall, the *Death and Assumption of the Virgin* (the composition of this work was later much copied by other artists).

The subjects from the *Life of St John the Baptist* on the right wall include (lower register) the *Angel appearing to St Zacharias in the Temple*, one of Domenico's last works in the chapel. In the group of men behind the angel, the one closest to the angel was almost certainly meant to be a portrait of the donor Giovanni Tornabuoni, and there are more Tornabuoni family portraits in the group on the right. In the group of three-quarter length figures below to the left, the portraits of famous humanist scholars including Poliziano and Ficino have been identified. The inscription above the arch on the right, dated 1490, exalts the splendour of Florence at this moment in its history. The splendid classical building is elaborately decorated with 'sculpted' relief and marble panels.

In the adjoining scene of the *Visitation* the most elegantly

dressed girl is probably Gio-
vanna degli Albizi who married Lorenzo Tornabuoni, son
of Giovanni, in 1486. This is
one of the most beautiful
scenes in the chapel, and includes the charming detail of
three men with their backs to
us leaning over a wall and ad-
miring the view. Domenico
may have included his self
portrait in the man climbing
the steps.

On the next register, in the
Birth of the Baptist the prominent figure of a girl carrying a
dish of fruit on her head is
copied from a similar figure in
a relief of the same subject by
Antonio del Pollaiolo on the
silver altar made for the Baptistery (now in the Museo del-
l'Opera del Duomo).

The *Naming of the Baptist* is in part by Sebastiano Mainardi,
except for the group of four men around the Baptist's father St
Zacharias, which are extremely well painted and are therefore
thought to be by Domenico himself. The upper scenes of the
Preaching of the Baptist, the *Baptism of Christ*, and the *Ban-
quet of Herod* (in the lunette at the top of the wall), although
composed by Domenico were probably painted largely by his
assistants.

Antonio del Pollaiolo,
Birth of the Baptist,
detail. Florence, Museo
dell'Opera del Duomo

From top down:
*The Angel appearing
to St Zacharias*;
Visitation; *Birth of the
Baptist*

SANTA TRINITA

Cappella Sassetti

The other famous fresco cycle by Ghirlandaio in Florence is the one in the Cappella Sassetti. It illustrates the *Life of St Francis* and was commissioned in 1483 by Francesco Sassetti, a merchant and manager of the Medici bank, another typical figure of Renaissance Florence. The frescoed decoration includes two large lunettes on the wall outside the chapel connected by a tall painted pilaster crowned with a statue of David : in one of the lunettes is the *Sibyl announcing the coming of Christ to Augustus*. These scenes had been painted over in the 18th century and were only rediscovered in the 1870s. Inside the chapel, on the vault, are four *Sibyls*, thought by some scholars to have been painted by Sebastiano Mainardi.

On the altar wall are two large spacious scenes, amongst Ghirlandaio's best works. In the lunette, *St Francis receives the Rule of the Order from Pope Honorius* set in Piazza della Signoria, with the Loggia dei Lanzi and Palazzo Vecchio prominent. Those present include (standing in the right foreground) Lorenzo il Magnifico (in profile) with the donor Francesco Sassetti and his son Federigo, and Antonio Pucci, one of the ruling magistrates of the city. Sassetti indicates the three young men standing on the opposite side of the lunette who are thought to be portraits of his three eldest sons. In this scene Ghirlandaio has introduced the very unusual element of a staircase in the foreground: ascending the steps are Agnolo Poliziano leading Lorenzo il Magnifico's sons Giuliano (as a young boy), Piero, and Giovanni. The delightful scene beneath of the *Miracle of the Boy brought back to Life* takes place in Piazza Santa Trinita (the church still has its romanesque façade and Ponte Santa Trinita has not yet been rebuilt). In the background the boy, who was the son of a Roman notary, can be seen falling to his death from a window of Palazzo Spini, and in the foreground is the lonely figure of the little boy in the centre of the composition,

St Francis receives the Rule of the Order, and detail (page 137)

who has just been brought back to life by St Francis (a posthumous miracle). The kneeling women who are half hidden below his bed, taken aback with fright to see him sitting up, are a charming detail. Numerous portraits are also included in this scene and some of them have been identified as Sassetti's five daughters (on the left), and members of the Florentine aristocracy such as Palla Strozzi, Maso degli Albizi, Neri di Gino Capponi. The figure on the extreme right (looking towards the spectator) may be a self-portrait and the figure next to him could represent Sebastiano Mainardi.

Miracle of the Boy brought back to Life, and detail

The magnificent painted altarpiece of the chapel, showing the *Adoration of the Shepherds*, also by Domenico, has exquisite details such as the bullfinch and stones (symbolizing the name Sassetti: *sasso* means stone) and a solitary iris in the foreground, and the Roman sarcophagus used as a manger, on the pilaster above which is the date 1483-85. The painting is flanked by the frescoed figures of the donors, *Francesco Sassetti and Nera Corsi,* his wife, kneeling in adoration, arranged as if in a triptych (Ghirlandaio was clearly influenced here by

Funeral of St Francis

the Flemish *Portinari Triptych*, now in the Uffizi). The date beneath the two donors (1495) records the year the frescoes and altarpiece were finished. On the walls the subjects are: *St Francis being tried by Fire before the Sultan*, and the *Funeral of St Francis*, the composition of both of which owes much to Giotto's frescoes in the Bardi Chapel in Santa Croce. The Funeral scene is particularly well painted, and includes on the extreme left two men in red hats who are thought to represent the Humanist scholars Poliziano and Bartolomeo Fonzio. The figures in red on the extreme right may, instead, be Sassetti with his two sons named Teodoro (the eldest died before the birth of the youngest). The scene of *St Francis receiving the Stigmata* includes views of La Verna and Pisa. *St Francis renouncing his Worldly Goods* was probably painted by Domenico's brother Davide.

Portraits of Nera Corsi and Francesco Sassetti Above: *Adoration of the Shepherds*

The decoration of the very well preserved chapel, which contains numerous references to classical antiquity, is completed with the two black porphyry sarcophagi, which serve as the tombs of the donors, the delicate carving of which is attributed to Giuliano da Sangallo.

PALAZZO VECCHIO

Sala dei Gigli

There is an important fresco by Ghirlandaio in the
Sala dei Gigli, one of the last
rooms to be visited on the upper floor of Palazzo Vecchio.
It is the only one carried out in
this room of the series which
were to have been commis-
sioned from other artists in-
cluding Botticelli and Perugino for the other walls. Ghirlandaio's fresco, dating from 1482, is a celebration of the Florentine
Republic. It is very well preserved, although it was unfortunately irreparably damaged in the late 16th century when the
marble doorway into the Sala delle Carte Geografiche was constructed. The three painted arches have six medallions of Roman emperors in the spandrels, and there is a painted relief
sculpture of the *Madonna and Child with two Angels* on a 'mosaic' ground. *St Zenobius* is enthroned between *Saints Stephen
and Lawrence* (or the deacons Eugenius and Cicero) in an open
loggia behind which there is a glimpse of the Duomo. The two
lions of Florence (the Marzocco) hold the flags of the 'Popolo'
and the 'Comune'. Above are two lunettes with six heroes of
ancient Rome.

The room takes its name from the delightful golden irises, the
symbol of Florence, which are incorporated into the decoration
of the magnificent carved wood ceiling (by Giuliano da Maiano, with whom Ghirlandaio is known to have collaborated in
other works). Irises were then painted on the walls, against a
dark blue ground, copying the background of Ghirlandaio's
fresco.

OGNISSANTI

Cenacolo

Ghirlandaio also frescoed a number of Last Suppers (*Cena-
coli*) in the refectories of Florentine convents between
1476 and 1480, the most beautiful of which is the Cenacolo of

Deposition; Madonna of the Misericordia

Also in this church are two very early frescoes by Ghirlandaio of a *Deposition* or *Pietà* and a *Madonna of the Misericordia* commissioned by the Vespucci family. The Madonna is shown protecting the Vespucci. Amerigo is supposed to be the young boy whose head appears between the Madonna and the man in the dark cloak.

Ognissanti. It is in a convent which has been occupied by Observant Franciscan friars since 1561 on the left of the church of Ognissanti. Off the 15th century cloister, with early 17th century frescoes of the *Life of St Francis* by Jacopo Ligozzi and others, is the pretty vaulted refectory on the end wall of which is the fresco of the *Last Supper*. When it was detached in 1966 its sinopia was found beneath and this is now displayed on the opposite wall. The room is filled with natural light from the windows and it is usually very peaceful and a delightful place to examine Ghirlandaio's skills as a fresco painter. By painting also the last two vaults of the room above the lunettes he projected the scene into the room itself.

It is dated 1480 beside Judah's left foot. The trees and plants and birds in the background are all Christian symbols, and even the fruits on the table such as the apricots and cherries were intended as references to Redemption through the sacrifice of Christ. The beautifully embroidered table cloth may have been a tribute to the friars who were for centuries known for their skills in cloth manufacturing. The Apostles are each depicted in an attitude of astonishment at the words of Christ, who is shown at the moment in which he indicates that one of them is to betray him. The head of Christ is strikingly different from the portrait heads of the Apostles and, as the difference in the sinopia shows, this was not, in fact, the head painted by Ghirlandaio but was repainted by Carlo Dolci in a 17th century restoration. It is likely that Leonardo recalled this work when he began his famous *Cenacolo* in Milan.

St Jerome in his Study

In the church of Ognissanti there is another fresco painted in the same year by Ghirlandaio of *St Jerome in his Study* now

displayed in the nave opposite a similar fresco by Botticelli of *St Augustine in his Study*, both of which originally decorated the choir screen of the church. Ghirlandaio's work is dated on the desk 1480. The green curtain in the background is a reminder that libraries and places of study in the 15th century normally had green walls since this colour was considered an encouragement to peaceful meditation. The exquisite detail of the objects on the desk and shelf including the saint's spectacles recall contemporary Flemish works, and the various inscriptions are in Latin, Greek, or Hebrew.

MUSEO DI SAN MARCO

Cenacolo

In the small refectory of the Convent of San Marco there is another *Cenacolo* by Ghirlandaio and his workshop which has great similarities to the Ognissanti work and is preserved in excellent condition. The composition was painted by Ghirlandaio, probably with the help of Davide Ghirlandaio and Sebastiano Mainardi. It has recently been put forward that this work may have been made some years before and not after the *Cenacolo* of Ognissanti. This can be visited regularly as it is part of the Museo di San Marco.

BADIA A PASSIGNANO

Outside Florence, at Badia a Passignano there is another *Cenacolo* by Ghirlandaio which is dated around 1456-57.

GALLERIA DEGLI UFFIZI

Madonna Enthroned with Saints

Adoration of the Magi

Three very fine altarpieces by Ghirlandaio are preserved in the Uffizi and are now exhibited in the room which contains numerous masterpieces by Botticelli. Two of them depict the *Madonna Enthroned with Saints*, and the third is a tondo of the *Adoration of the Magi*. This is mentioned by Vasari as being in the house of Giovanni Tornabuoni, Ghirlandaio's patron.

SPEDALE DEGLI INNOCENTI

Adoration of the Magi

There is another extremely beautiful *Adoration of the Magi* in the Pinacoteca of the Spedale degli Innocenti in Piazza Santissima Annunziata. This was commissioned for the high al-

tar of the church by the prior Francesco Tesori who died in 1497 and whose tomb slab has been placed in the floor in front of the painting. The brightly coloured composition includes a scene of the Massacre of the Innocents and two child saints in the foreground, an obvious reference to the foundling hospital here. The donor and the artist are portrayed amongst the courtiers attending the Kings. The predella is by Bartolomeo di Giovanni.

SANT'ANDREA (Cercina)

Saints Jerome, Barbara and Anthony Abbot

Just outside Florence in the lovely country church of Sant' Andrea at Cercina in the hills above Careggi a fresco of *Saints Jerome, Barbara and Anthony Abbot* is probably Ghirlandaio's earliest fresco of all. It was discovered in 1923 and shows the influence of Domenico Veneziano. Ghirlandaio's family had property in this area which is still particularly beautiful and well worth visiting (numerous walks can be taken along the country lanes here).

DUOMO

Annunciation

In 1491 Ghirlandaio designed the lunette mosaic of the *Annunciation* (executed by his brother Davide) above the Porta della Mandorla of the Duomo, on the north side of the church. He also provided the cartoon for a stained glass window in the third north chapel of Santa Maria Maddalena dei Pazzi. This was a commission from Lorenzo Tornabuoni (son of Giovanni who had ordered the fresco cycle in Santa Maria Novella from Ghirlandaio).

MICHELANGELO BUONARROTI

Recognized by his contemporaries as the most important painter, sculptor and architect of his time, Michelangelo has remained an almost mythical figure in succeeding centuries, and no other artist has ever received so much critical attention. He lived to a great age and produced numerous masterpieces, including the Sistine chapel frescoes in Rome, and the world famous sculpture of *David* in Florence, and has also fascinated generations of scholars through his writings and drawings which reveal an exceptionally complex and tormented character. Although he left some of his greatest works in Rome, and lived there for the last thirty years of his life, he always considered himself a Florentine and his heir and nephew Lionardo saw to it that at his death his body was returned to his native city, where the 'divine Michelangelo' was given a funeral service in San Lorenzo, the grandest that has ever been awarded to any Florentine, before his burial in Santa Croce. There is no doubt that Michelangelo's art was in many ways a culmination of the Florentine Renaissance.

Michelangelo was born in 1475 in the tiny little Tuscan village of Caprese, now called Caprese Michelangelo, since his father had been sent there as 'podestà', but after just one month the family

Marcello Venusti, *Portrait of Michelangelo*. Florence, Casa Buonarroti

moved back to Florence. His contemporary biographers (Condivi and Vasari) both relate the story that Michelangelo often fondly pointed out that he was nursed in Settignano by a woman who was the daughter and wife of a stonemason, and so he supposed that it was through her that he 'inherited' his gifts as a sculptor. He was the second of five children, and his mother died when he was only six.

Although his father was opposed to him taking up a career as an artist, his talents were obvious from a very early age, and at fourteen he joined Domenico Ghirlandaio's workshop where he excelled as a particularly precocious pupil. At that time Ghirlandaio was at work on the fresco cycle in the choir of Santa Maria Novella. Another painter, who was also Ghirlandaio's pupil, Francesco Granacci, pointed out his talents to Lorenzo il Magnifico and suggested he join the group of young artists protected by Lorenzo who worked under the direction of Bertoldo in the garden of San Marco. Bertoldo, who had been a pupil of Donatello's, and was an expert bronze caster and friend of Lorenzo's, was by now probably too old to work himself but there apparently taught promising young sculptors and oversaw the restoration of antique sculpture. Lorenzo was quick to recognize Michelangelo's exceptional skills and obtained his father's

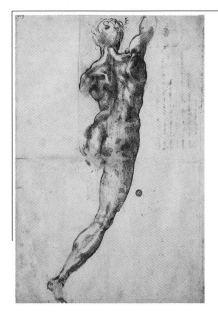

Michelangelo, Study of a nude figure for *The Battle of Cascina*. Florence, Casa Buonarroti

permission for him to come and live in the Medici household. Michelangelo stayed there for the last years of Lorenzo's life, and thus came into contact with the Humanists Poliziano, Pico della Mirandola and Marsilio Ficino. At the age of seventeen, on Lorenzo's death, he returned home, but kept on good terms with Lorenzo's son Piero, who during an exceptional snowfall asked Michelangelo to make a snowman for him in the courtyard of Palazzo Medici! All his life he was to remain closely linked with the Medici, although his complicated relationship with them went through alternate phases, since he was at heart a Republican and supporter of Savonarola.

As a young man it is known that he made careful studies (since his drawings survive) of the frescoes by Masaccio and Giotto in Florence.

His biographers mention that after Lorenzo's death Michelangelo bought an abandoned piece of marble and sculpted a colossal Hercules (now lost). This is considered particularly significant since the work was not a commission, and is one of the first cases known where a sculptor decided to carve something for himself, simply for the joy of doing so. Indeed in his writings Michelangelo declared that he was a painter and sculptor for his own honour and that of his family.

At around the age of eighteen he managed to persuade the prior of Santo Spirito to let him study anatomy through the dissection of corpses and this helped him to portray the human body with such remarkable precision, while at the same time he came face to face with the reality of death. For religious reasons an opportunity of this kind was extremely difficult to obtain.

He went to Rome in 1500 and there carved his first masterpiece, *Bacchus* (now in the Bargello museum), and when he returned to Florence he received his first important commission from the Comune of Florence, his marble *David* which immediately established him as the greatest sculptor of his age. His fame quickly spread, and in 1504 he was ordered by Pier Soderini to paint a scene of the *Battle of Cascina* on the wall of the Salone dei Cinquecento in Palazzo Vecchio opposite another battle scene by Leonardo da Vinci. Michelangelo's composition was to illustrate the battle (1364) in which the Florentine soldiers who had set up camp at Cascina just outside Pisa fought without armour since they had taken it off to have a swim in the Arno on an exceptionally hot day, and were only just saved from defeat since one of their company saw the Pisans approaching and gave the alarm. The scene therefore provided Michelangelo with ample scope to demonstrate his skill in portraying the nude male body as well as figures in action. However he only produced the cartoon for this work and probably never actually began the fresco. The cartoon was studied and copied by numerous artists and it eventually got torn and divided up into many pieces. Although, as Condivi relates, it was "preserved with great diligence as something sacred", in the end none of it survived. Only a few sketches by Michelangelo are preserved at the Casa Buonarroti and the Uffizi which were studies made for this work. When Cellini saw the cartoon he commented: "never among the ancients or the moderns was so high and noble a work seen", and Vasari describes it in great detail.

Numerous letters have survived which

prove that Michelangelo always remained closely attached to his family, and his heir, his nephew Lionardo, carefully preserved some of his works and the house which Michelangelo bought in 1508 in Via Ghibellina. Lionardo's son, Michelangelo, made this into a 'shrine' in memory of his great-uncle which exists to this day as a fascinating and beautifully kept little museum, the Casa Buonarroti. Here are preserved two of Michelangelo's works made while still a boy (the *Battle of the Centaurs* and the *Madonna of the Steps*) which clearly demonstrate his remarkable skills as a sculptor. The *Madonna of the Steps* was owned by his nephew Lionardo, who donated it to Cosimo I in 1566 (but in 1616 it was given back to the family and has been in the Casa Buonarroti ever since). The *Battle* relief, instead, seems never to have left this house. It is interesting to note that neither of these very early works is totally finished.

Both works illustrate Michelangelo's debt to Donatello and Bertoldo and also show the influence of ancient classical art on his work. Vasari relates that one day a Florentine noticed Michelangelo studying Donatello's statue of *St Mark* on the outside of Orsanmichele and asked him his opinion of it, to which Michelangelo replied that he had never seen a "statue with more of the air of nobility about it, and if St Mark were like that, one could well believe the things that he has written". It has also recently been recognized that the marble sculptures of Benedetto da Maiano (including his unfinished *St Sebastian* which he left to the Compagnia del Bigallo and is now in the Oratory of the Misericordia in Piazza del Duomo) must have had an influence on the young Michelangelo.

His most famous work in Florence, the colossal marble *David*, has become in many ways the symbol of the city and a cult image which draws crowds of visitors to the Galleria dell'Accademia every year, even if it is maybe not his masterpiece. Here, too, are kept the remarkably powerful unfinished sculptures of the *Slaves* made for the tomb of Julius II in Rome. Other very fine sculptural works by him in Florence, nowadays much less famous but equally fascinating are pres-

Benedetto da Maiano, *St Sebastian*, Florence, Oratorio della Misericordia

Michelangelo, *Dying Slave*. Paris, Louvre

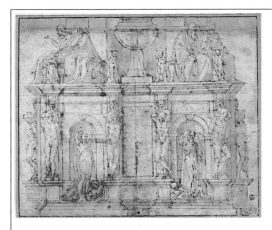

Michelangelo, Project for the tomb of Julius II.
Florence, Gabinetto dei Disegni e delle Stampe
degli Uffizi

commission, or had to leave Florence at a certain stage for political reasons, such as the expulsion of the Medici or the siege of Florence in 1529. But as Vasari so aptly says, when describing his *Madonna and Child* in the Sagrestia Nuova: "...even though its parts are not finished, having been roughed out and left showing the marks of the chisel, in the imperfect block one recognizes the perfection of the work". One of the most important scholars of Michelangelo in the 20th century, Charles De Tolnay, also suggested that Michelangelo may have at times been hesitant to complete his works because of "his awareness that to free the figure from the block completely would have necessarily involved his own detachment from the material stone, that is to say the destruction of the evidence for the process of creation". His most obviously unfinished works, the four *Slaves* and the *St Matthew* in the Galleria dell'Accademia were left unfinished for specific historic reasons: the *Slaves* because the tomb of Julius II was finally abandoned, and the *St Matthew* because Michelangelo's contract with the Opera del Duomo for twelve statues of the Apostles was cancelled by them in 1505. However, all Michelangelo's unfinished sculptures are superb works and in no way are they less beautiful because of their unfinished state. It is obvious that he did not intentionally leave them unfinished as was often the case with sculptors who worked many centuries later.

In these works one can see most clearly Michelangelo's unique concept, expressed in his poetry, that the sculpture already existed within the block of stone, and it is the sculptor's job merely to take away what is superfluous. But it is also apparent, as Enzo Carli suggested, that in order to 'liberate' his images from the block of marble Michelangelo seems to have been involved in a titanic struggle. The way in which Michelangelo confronted his task, as Cellini noted, was to begin from a frontal viewpoint, as if

erved in the Bargello museum and Palazzo Vecchio. But Florence also owns the only finished panel painting by Michelangelo, the *Tondo Doni* in the Uffizi, and his most elaborate and eccentric architectural works, the Sagrestia Nuova with the Medici tombs in San Lorenzo and the Biblioteca Laurenziana, the former also containing his most important group of sculptures.

Michelangelo had an immediate and lasting effect on all contemporary artists, and in many ways changed the course of all three arts in Europe. Florence is also one of the best places to study this influence through the works of the Mannerists. However, it has been suggested by some art historians, that Michelangelo's influence was so overpowering that it may perhaps have also had a somewhat damaging effect on his followers, as it tended to stifle any other artistic currents at work (Cellini, although himself a great admirer of Michelangelo, stands out as the most striking example of a Florentine artist who managed to work in a style very different from that of Michelangelo at a time when the work of almost every other sculptor could be defined as 'Michelangelesque').

Since so many of Michelangelo's works are unfinished, art historians have debated for centuries the significance of his 'non-finito', and why some of his works were left at an unfinished stage. In most cases they were left unfinished because he was called away to some new carving a high relief, and thus the statue gradually emerged from the marble. Vasari also tries to explain this process by suggesting that the sculpture could be likened to a figure placed in a tub of water and then gradually lifted towards the surface. It is known that Michelangelo made very little use of a pantograph, which was the normal method by which other sculptors proceeded in their works. In almost all his sculptures the characteristic marks of Michelangelo's toothed chisel (or *gradina*) can be seen, which recall the 'hatching' made by his pen in his drawings: thus his drawings seem to have the signs of his sculptures and his sculptures, especially those left unfinished, seem to be 'drawn'.

Michelangelo's poetry as well as his art explored the principles of Platonic aesthetics. There is always a strong element of drama and often desperation in his works, which seems to portray the intimate complexity of the human soul and its ultimately tragic destiny. It is known from his writings that he had an innate fear of old age and death, and the Medici tombs in San Lorenzo are often interpreted as an allegory of the brevity of human life. His contemporaries referred to the "terribilità" in his works, a word which sums up their extraordinary power as well as the elements of despair which they contain.

Much of Michelangelo's life was taken up with the tormented commission for the tomb of Julius II, which he failed to complete, and which apparently led him to come close to a breakdown. It seems that the accusations made against him recounted by Vasari that he may have been dishonest in accepting advance payments for this work and that it was due to him rather than the Popes that the sculptures for the tomb were delayed and finally abandoned, led to his request to Condivi to write his biography which in part refutes Vasari's less favourable version of the story. Vasari, however, knew Michelangelo well, and he was the only living and fully active artist whose life Vasari chose to describe in his famous *Vite*.

The *Pietà* preserved in the Museo dell'Opera del Duomo in Florence is Michelangelo's last important work (except for his touching *Pietà Rondanini*, reworked by another hand). At one time he intended this to be used for his own tomb and it seems he identified himself with the figure of Nicodemus (apparently a self-portrait). This converted Pharisee is supposed to have been present at the burial of Christ. Michelangelo worked on this particularly moving work at the very end of his life (he died in 1564), when he told Vasari that "exercising with the chisel kept his body healthy".

Agostino Ciampelli,
*Funeral of
Michelangelo in
San Lorenzo.* Florence,
Casa Buonarroti

MUSEO DELL'OPERA DEL DUOMO

Pietà

This sculptural group is a very beautiful late work, probably carved when he was in his late 70s or even early 80s, and the head of Nicodemus is supposed to be a self-portrait. The anguished face of the Madonna is unfinished. The sculpture combines the portrayal of a Pietà scene with that of a Deposition and Entombment. Michelangelo once intended this sculpture be used for his own tomb when he thought he would be buried in Rome, but he then apparently decided instead to ask to be buried in Florence, and so in 1561 sold the sculpture to Francesco Bandini, who installed it in his garden in Rome. Bandini was a friend of Tiberio Calcagni, who was a young Florentine sculptor and architect who frequented Michelangelo's circle. Apparently dissatisfied with his work, and partly in anger since the marble proved defective, Michelangelo had destroyed the left arm and leg of Christ in 1555, and Bandini asked Calcagni to repair the arm and finish the figure of Mary Magdalen for him. Calcagni had also completed Michelangelo's *Bust of Brutus*, and helped him prepare the drawings and models for the church of San Giovanni dei Fiorentini in Rome. He died aged 33 just two years after his master.

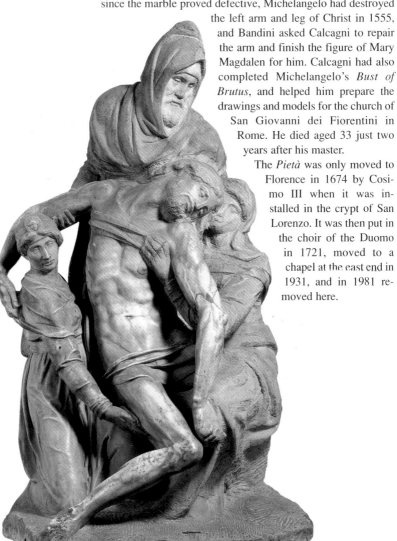

The *Pietà* was only moved to Florence in 1674 by Cosimo III when it was installed in the crypt of San Lorenzo. It was then put in the choir of the Duomo in 1721, moved to a chapel at the east end in 1931, and in 1981 removed here.

PALAZZO VECCHIO

Victory

This statue is probably the least famous work by Michelangelo in Florence, often overlooked by tourists. It was made during his last Florentine period probably for a niche in the ill-fated tomb of Julius II in Rome. A strongly knit two-figure group, intended as one of a pair, the serpentine form of the principal figure was frequently copied by later Mannerist sculptors. Left in Michelangelo's Florentine studio at his death, it was presented to Cosimo I by Michelangelo's nephew Lionardo a year later, and set up here by Vasari as a celebration of the victory of Cosimo I over Siena. It may originally have been intended as an allegory of the Victory of Youth over Old Age, or Virtue overcoming Vice. The statue was left unpolished by Michelangelo.

It was for this room that Michelangelo made a cartoon for a fresco of the *Battle of Cascina* between Florence and Pisa which was to have been painted opposite a huge mural begun by Leonardo da Vinci the year before representing the Florentine victory at Anghiari over Milan in 1440. Leonardo experimented, without success, with a new technique of mural painting and completed only a fragment of the work before leaving Florence for Milan in 1506. It is not known whether this had disappeared or was destroyed (probably by order of Cosimo I) before the present frescoes were carried out under the direction of Vasari. Michelangelo probably only completed the cartoon and never began his fresco since he was called to Rome by Pope Julius II. However some scholars still believe there could be traces of these two works of fundamental importance to artists of the time beneath the present decorations.

GALLERIA DEGLI UFFIZI

Tondo Doni

This is the only finished painting known by Michelangelo, and it is executed in tempera. It shows the Holy Family in a very unusual composition, with the seated Madonna, having just finished reading, handing the Child to Joseph behind her. The significance of the classical male nude figures sitting on a wall in the background has been much discussed: they are sometimes interpreted as prophetic figures or references to the Christian sacrament of baptism, or even as symbols of paganism. One of them, behind Joseph, seems to have a pose inspired by the classical sculpture of the *Laocoön*, which was found in Rome in 1506. Once thought to have been a wedding gift for Agnolo Doni and his wife Maddalena Strozzi, the tondo is now usually dated a few years later probably around 1507, and could have been given to them on the occasion of the birth of their daughter Maria. Although owing something to tondoes of the same subject by Luca Signorelli, a very fine example of which can be seen in the Uffizi, it signalled a new moment in High Renaissance painting, and pointed the way forward to the Sistine chapel frescoes. It was arguably the most important panel painting of the 16th century, and from 1653 was displayed in a place of honour in the Tribuna of the Uffizi. When the painting was cleaned in the 1986 the luminous vibrant colours were returned to its surface. The splendid contemporary frame, with busts of Christ, two prophets, and two angels is by Domenico del Tasso.

Agesandros, Polydoros and Athenodoros of Rhodes, *Laocoön*. Vatican, Museo Pio Clementino

GALLERIA DELL'ACCADEMIA

The four Slaves

These are perhaps Michelangelo's most powerful sculptures, particularly extraordinary because of their unfinished state, some of them barely blocked out. They were made for the tomb of Julius II which was never completed, but their date is uncertain, and they were still in Michelangelo's studio in Florence at the time of his death (his nephew Lionardo donated them to Cosimo I in 1564). Also called the 'prisoners' they show four strong male figures seeming to struggle free of the stone in

Slave, known as *Atlas*

Dying Slave. Paris, Louvre

Rebellious Slave. Paris, Louvre

Bearded Slave   *Young Slave*   *Awakening Slave*

which they are 'imprisoned' and in no other works can Michelangelo's method of sculpting be more clearly seen. They may have been intended as Atlas figures or caryatids but what their final appearance would have been is only conjectural. In 1585 they were put in the Grotta del Buontalenti in the Boboli gardens, and only moved here in 1908. Two famous smaller *Slaves* were made for an earlier project of the tomb: these were in France by the mid 16th century and are now in the Louvre.

St Matthew

This is another unfinished work, still little more than a relief, showing Michelangelo's technique of sculpting from a frontal viewpoint, intent on taking away what is superfluous in the block of marble which already seems to contain his finished statue. It is an early but extraordinarily powerful work (c 1503) and was one of the twelve Apostles commissioned by the Opera del Duomo from Michelangelo, and the only one he ever began (the contract was annulled in 1505). The other statues were then commissioned from Michelangelo's followers, including Baccio Bandinelli, Vincenzo de' Rossi and Andrea Sansovino (and are now to be seen against the piers of the octagon of the Duomo). The *St Matthew* remained on the premises of the Opera del Duomo until 1834.

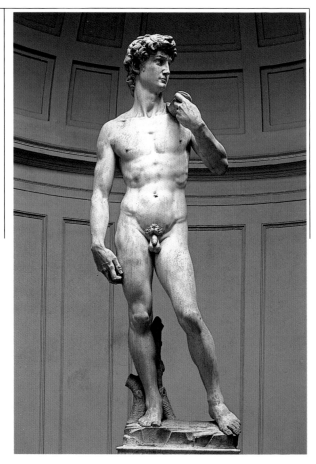

Daniele da Volterra
Bust of Michelangelo

This bronze bust is
thought to be one of
the most accurate
portraits of
Michelangelo,
sculpted by his pupil.
As one of his closest
friends, Daniele was
present at the death of
his master.

David

This is perhaps now the most famous single work of art of western civilisation, and has become something of a cult image, all too familiar through endless reproductions, although it is not the work by which Michelangelo is best judged.

It was commissioned by the city of Florence in 1501 and, when it was nearly finished, a committee was set up to decide where it should be exhibited (both Botticelli and Andrea della Robbia were members). Their decision was to install it against the rough stone wall of Palazzo Vecchio where its huge scale fitted its setting. Here in the Galleria dell'Accademia it seems out of place in a cold heroic niche in a tribune specially built by Emilio De Fabris in 1882 to exhibit it when it was removed from Piazza della Signoria.

The colossal block of marble, some 5 metres high, quarried in 1464 for the Opera del Duomo, had been left abandoned in the cathedral workshop. The marble was offered to several other artists, including Andrea Sansovino and Leonardo da Vinci, before it was finally assigned to Michelangelo. The figure of David, uncharacteristic of Michelangelo's works, stands in a classical pose derived from antique statues and suited to the shallow block of marble. The hero, a young colossus, called by Michelangelo's contemporaries 'il gigante', is shown in the

moment before his victory over Goliath. It is probable that Michelangelo was asked to take as his model Donatello's famous bronze statue of *David*. A celebration of the nude, the statue established Michelangelo at the age of 29 as the foremost sculptor of his time, when it was inaugurated in 1504. In 1527 when the Medici were exiled from Florence, the left arm of the statue was broken in three pieces, but it was repaired by Vasari and Francesco Salviati. The second toe of the left foot was broken by a vandal in 1991 but has been restored. There are two replicas of the statue in Florence, one in its original position outside Palazzo Vecchio, and one in bronze surrounded by copies of his other famous marble statues in the city, set up in Piazzale Michelangelo in 1875. During the Second World War this sculpture, together with those of the *Slaves* was protected by a 'dome' of bricks since, because of their weight, they could not be removed quickly enough from Florence for safety with the many other works of art which were put in secret store-places outside the city.

SAN LORENZO

Balcony of the Holy Relics

T his is a very little known and minor work by Michelangelo in Florence. Above the west door, it is a small balcony supported by two columns in pietra serena which was used for the exhibition of the Holy Relics which belonged to the church and were kept in a treasury behind the three little doors. Pope Clement VII asked Michelangelo to design this in 1530, and it was finished by 1532. The Medici family gave permission to the Accademia delle Arti del Disegno to hold Michelangelo's

elaborate funeral service in this, their family church. It was organized by Vasari and Vincenzo Borghini, prior of the Spedale degli Innocenti, and Cosimo I asked Benedetto Varchi, the court rhetorician, to give the funeral oration.

CAPPELLE MEDICEE

Sagrestia Nuova

B oth the chapel and the Medici tombs were designed by Michelangelo, but they were left unfinished by him when he departed from Florence for the last time for Rome in 1534 in anger at the political climate in the city. The so-called New Sacristy may have been begun by Giuliano da Sangallo c 1491, but it was continued by Michelangelo in 1520-24 for Cardinal Giulio de' Medici (elected Pope Clement VII in 1523). Work was interrupted with the expulsion of the Medici, but resumed in 1530-33. It balances Brunelleschi's Old Sacristy in the church of San Lorenzo and drew inspiration from it, but was used from its inception as a funerary chapel for the Medici family. As in the Old Sacristy the architectural features are emphasized by the use of dark grey pietra serena, but the design is severe and idiosyncratic, breaking totally with classical forms and early Renaissance canons. It produces a strange, cold atmosphere, in part due to the diffusion of light exclusively from above, and the odd perspective devices on the upper parts of the walls. The coffered ceiling, which was formerly decorated with stuccoes by Giovanni da Udine, but altered by Vasari, has been recently restored. The small room has no less than eight doors, only four of which could be used as such, beneath empty niches. The architectural details are extremely refined and the carving of the friezes and cor-

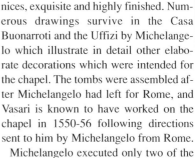

nices, exquisite and highly finished. Numerous drawings survive in the Casa Buonarroti and the Uffizi by Michelangelo which illustrate in detail other elaborate decorations which were intended for the chapel. The tombs were assembled after Michelangelo had left for Rome, and Vasari is known to have worked on the chapel in 1550-56 following directions sent to him by Michelangelo from Rome.

Michelangelo executed only two of the famous Medici tombs, out of the three or more originally projected (and which were originally intended to stand in the centre of the chapel). To the left of the entrance is the *Tomb of Lorenzo, Duke of Urbino* (1492-1519), grandson of Lorenzo il Magnifico. The statue of the Duke shows him seated, absorbed in meditation, dressed in classical armour, with a lion's mask on his helmet. On the sarcophagus below are a pair of reclining figures representing *Dawn* as a young girl and *Dusk* as a middle-aged man in deep thought. Opposite is the *Tomb of Giuliano, Duke of Nemours* (1479-1516), the third son of Lorenzo il Magnifico. Beneath are the allegorical sculptures of *Day* and *Night*. The elegant reclining female figure of *Night*, with the symbols of darkness (the moon, an owl, and a mask), is considered to be among the finest of all Michelangelo's sculptures. Its pose recalls antique sculptures of Leda. The male figure which represents *Day*, with its head hardly worked on at

Tomb of Lorenzo, Duke of Urbino, and detail showing Dawn

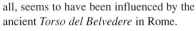

Tomb of Giuliano,
Duke of Nemours, and
detail showing *Night*

all, seems to have been influenced by the ancient *Torso del Belvedere* in Rome.

Both Lorenzo and Giuliano, comparatively insignificant members of the Medici family, had both died young leaving no heirs. Although Giuliano is praised in Baldassarre Castiglione's *Courtier* and Macchiavelli dedicated his *Prince* to Lorenzo, who, however died insane, it is only their tombs that have ensured their fame. They are shown with idealized portraits, but as living people, rather than through effigies. It has been suggested that the sculptures could have been intended also as allegories of active and contemplative life, but discussions continue amongst art historians over the precise significance of the various elements in the chapel which also seem to refer to the inevitable passage of time and its destructive force, in opposition to the immortality of the soul. It is interesting to note that none of the eyes of the figure sculptures here have carved irises.

The entrance wall was intended to contain the architectural monument to Lorenzo il Magnifico and his brother Giuliano; the only part carried out by Michelangelo is the *Madonna and Child,* his last statue of a Madonna and one of his most beautiful. It was begun in 1521 but left unfinished in 1534. The figures on either side of *St Cosmas* and *St Damian*, the medical saints who were the patrons of the Medici, are by Giovannangelo da Montorsoli and Raffaello da Montelupo. Lorenzo il Magnifico's coffin was transferred here from the Old Sacristy in 1559.

The austere altar bears two candelabra, both designed by Michelangelo: the one on the left has particularly delicate carving by Silvio Cosini, and the one on the right was only made in 1741. On the walls behind the altar architectural graffiti were uncovered in the 1970s. Some of these are attributed to Michelangelo, and others to his followers, including Tribolo.

The door to the left of the altar gives access to a little room where charcoal drawings of great interest were discovered on the walls in 1975. The drawings aroused much discussion among art historians, most of whom recognized them as works by Michelangelo. The artist had supported the Republican government of Florence and helped erect fortifications on the hill of San Miniato to defend the city from the Medici Pope Clement VII and the Emperor. When the Medici returned in 1530 the Florentine governors issued an order calling for Michelangelo's execution, and so Michelangelo went into hiding

Day (above)
Detail showing Michelangelo's candelabrum on the altar (below)

until later in the year when Clement VII requested that he be treated with clemency. It is thought that he hid here for a time under the protection of his friend, the prior of San Lorenzo, and amused himself by making sketches on the walls. The drawings clearly refer to works by Michelangelo, such as his statue of Giuliano in the adjoining chapel. The large figure study for a *Resurrection of Christ* on the entrance wall is particularly remarkable.

Hundreds of drawings by Michelangelo, usually considered the greatest draughtsman of all times, survive in collections all over the world. These include preparatory studies for almost all his major commissions as well as highly finished 'presentation drawings'.

Study for the tomb of Giuliano, Duke of Nemours

Figure study for a Resurrection of Christ

Above left: *Madonna and Child*, and detail (page 166)

BIBLIOTECA LAURENZIANA

This library was begun by Michelangelo in 1524 on the order of Giulio de' Medici to house the collection of manuscripts made by Cosimo il Vecchio and Lorenzo il Magnifico. He worked on the library at the same time as the Sagrestia Nuova up until 1527 when the Medici were expelled from Florence. After the siege of Florence, when Michelangelo was in charge of the fortifications erected to defend the Republican government, and a period in hiding from the Medici in San Lorenzo (see above), he resumed work on the library until he finally left Florence for Rome in 1534.

The solemn vestibule, almost totally filled with an elaborate free-standing staircase was constructed by Vasari and Ammannati from Michelangelo's design in 1559-71 (correspondence survives to show that Michelangelo passed detailed plans and models on to Vasari in the 1550s). The staircase, as an architectural feature, was to be copied numerous times by later architects. A remarkable monument of Mannerist architecture, it has been interpreted by scholars in numerous different ways. It testifies to Michelangelo's sculptural conception of architecture, with a pronounced use of pietra serena in the tall room.

The peaceful reading room, a long hall, with, instead an unusually low ceiling, provides an unexpected contrast. Here the angle at which the architectural decoration can be seen has been carefully calculated, and the desks, also by Michelangelo, form an intricate part of the design. It is interesting to note that the heavily decorated vestibule is invisible from the aisle (only a blank wall is framed in the doorway). The wood ceiling and lovely terracotta floor are by Tribolo.

MUSEO NAZIONALE DEL BARGELLO

Bacchus

Michelangelo's first important statue, this was made on his first visit to Rome c 1497 perhaps for the banker, Jacopo Galli, who became an important patron of Michelangelo's, or for Cardinal Riario. It was kept in Galli's sculpture garden, which included some antique pieces, for over 50 years which accounts for its weathered surface, and was then purchased by Francesco de' Medici in 1571 and brought to Florence.

It shows the influence of classical works but at the same time portrays an extraordinary sense of imbalance due to Bacchus' drunken state. It is interesting to note that the cup he holds in his hand is a unique reinterpretation of an antique *skyphos*. The statue is quite unlike Michelangelo's later works. It was well described by Condivi in his *Life of Michelangelo* in 1553: "...the joyful face and the sullen and lascivious eyes, which seem to be those of one seized by the sovereign love of wine. In his right hand he holds a cup, like one who wants to drink, and he is looking at it like one who takes great pleasure in that liquor, which he himself invented; so he has a garland of vine-leaves on his head. On his left arm he has the skin of a tiger, an animal that is dedicated to him, as one that delights very much in grapes; it is only a skin and not the animal itself, to signify that whoever gives up his senses and his appetite to that fruit and that liquor will at last lose his life. In the hand of this arm he holds a bunch of grapes, which is being furtively nibbled by a little satyr at his feet, slender and jolly, who looks about seven years old; Bacchus himself looks about eighteen".

Apollo

A charming small statue in a typical *contrapposto* serpentine pose, this is another beautiful unpolished work by Michelangelo. Vasari describes it as Apollo attempting to extract an arrow from his back: "a most rare thing, still not completely finished", and states that it was carved for Baccio Valori (a Medici supporter who governed Florence) which would date it around 1530. It later formed part of the Medici collections (where it was referred to as a figure of David), and was moved to the Boboli gardens and later to the Uffizi where it was displayed amongst the antique sculptures.

Madonna and Child with the Infant St John (Tondo Pitti)

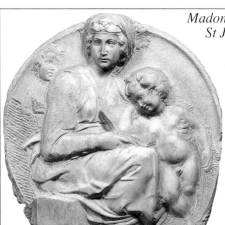

Made for Bartolomeo Pitti c 1503-05, this is a charming work. It later passed into the hands of the Guicciardini family, and in 1823 entered the Florentine public collections. The Child shows the influence of antique sculpture, and the figure of the Madonna is reminiscent of some of Jacopo della Quercia's sculptures. The *schiacciato* technique is derived from Donatello. But Michelangelo's genius can be detected in the unusual composition, with the Virgin's seat and her head interrupting the circular form, and the intense expressions of both the Virgin and the Child. Another very fine tondo of the *Madonna and Child*, which preceded this work, is now in the Royal Academy in London.

Madonna and Child.
London, Royal
Academy

Brutus

The only bust Michelangelo ever sculpted, this remarkable work is clearly derived from Imperial Roman portrait busts. Brutus has an extraordinarily powerful and sensual head which is turned forcefully to the left. It is a late work of uncertain date, once thought to have been made c 1539 soon after the murder of Duke Alessandro de' Medici by his cousin Lorenzino in 1537, but some scholars have now dated it later at the time of the violent death of Lorenzino himself (then in exile in Venice) in 1548.

It was made for Cardinal Niccolò Ridolfi as an exaltation of Republicanism, identifying Lorenzino with Brutus, Ceasar's assassin. The cardinal was a good friend of Michelangelo's and of his biographer Condivi, and all three were convinced Republicans. It was left unfinished and Tiberio Calcagni added the drapery. It was apparently acquired by the Medici in 1590.

CASA BUONARROTI

Three houses on this site were purchased in 1508 by Michelangelo. He left the property to his heir and only descendant, Lionardo, who united the houses into one building following a plan already drawn up by Michelangelo. In turn, his son, called Michelangelo, an art collector and man of letters, made part of the house into a gallery in 1612 as a memorial to his great-uncle. The last member of this branch of the Buonarroti family founded the present museum in 1858. It contains 16th century paintings and sculptures derived from works (some of them now lost) by Michelangelo. It also has 16th-19th century portraits of Michelangelo based on a prototype of c 1535 by Jacopino del Conte, also preserved here, as well as a well-known portrait of Michelangelo in a turban attributed to Giuliano Bugiardini, and a bronze head of the great artist by Daniele da Volterra.

The foundation which now administers the beautifully kept little Museum owns a very fine collection of original drawings by Michelangelo, which are displayed in rotation. The Galleria, decorated with statues and paintings in 1613-35 for Michelangelo Buonarroti the Younger, illustrates Michelangelo's life and apotheosis. There is also a room dedicated to the cult of Michelangelo in the 19th century.

Giuliano Bugiardini (attributed), *Portrait of Michelangelo in a Turban*

View of the Galleria in Casa Buonarroti

Model for the façade of San Lorenzo

This wooden model for the façade of San Lorenzo was made by Pietro Urbano following a design by Michelangelo. Drawings survive in the Casa Buonarroti illustrating the various projects made by Michelangelo over a number of years, and it seems this was not in fact his definitive design. Recalling a palace rather than a church façade, all at one height, it was to have been decorated with numerous sculptures. Leo X commissioned Michelangelo in 1516 to draw up a design, and his project was accepted in 1518. Despite the fact he was already at work on quarrying the marble, the contract was annulled, to Michelangelo's great annoyance and disappointment, on the death of Clement VII in 1520, and in fact the west front of the church remains bare to this day.

Drawing with a study for the façade of San Lorenzo. Casa Buonarroti

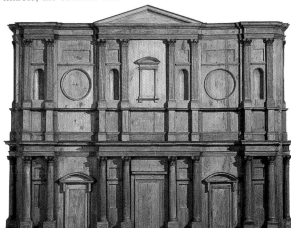

Madonna of the Steps

This relief is Michelangelo's first known work, carved at the age of 15 or 16. The low *schiacciato* relief shows the influence of Donatello. Vasari states that it had been given by Michelangelo's nephew Lionardo to Cosimo I, and then in 1616 Cosimo II gave it back to Lionardo's son Michelangelo the Younger in recognition for all he was doing to perpetuate his great-uncle's memory. The expression of the Madonna seems to foreshadow the death of Christ, and the putti in the background appear to be holding a funerary shroud.

Battle of the Centaurs

This relief is also one of Michelangelo's earliest works mentioned by both Vasari and Condivi, made when Michelangelo frequented the sculpture garden of San Marco, and carved just before the death of Lorenzo il Magnifico in 1492. He took up work on it again a few years later, but then left it unfinished. It was modelled on ancient sarcophagi (and in particular on one in the Camposanto at Pisa), and seems to represent a mythological battle between Greeks and centaurs, one of Ovid's favourite subjects, probably suggested to Michelangelo by Poliziano. Michelangelo's teacher, Bertoldo had already made a particularly fine battle relief in bronze (now in the Bargello museum), and it was recognized that such scenes were a test of an artist's skill in carving, and his ability to show the human figure in numerous different positions. It was almost certainly designed to be seen in a higher position than that in which it is at present displayed. At Michelangelo's death it was carefully preserved by his nephew Lionardo and has been in this house, where Vasari admired it, ever since.

VILLA MICHELANGELO (Settignano)

Charcoal drawing of a Triton or Satyr, attributed

It is known that Michelangelo spent his youth in this house which bears a commemorative plaque on the façade. In 1979 a charcoal drawing on the kitchen wall was detached and restored, and some scholars believe it is by Michelangelo. It was exhibited in the Casa Buonarroti in 1999.

Torso of a River God

This is probably a model for a colossal torso of a river god, one of four intended for the Sagrestia Nuova in San Loren-zo, but never carried out. Some scholars in the past have attrib-uted it instead to Ammannati. It is made of a mixture of wood, unfired clay, sand, animal fur or wool, plant fibres, and wire, and is particularly interesting as the only full-scale model by Michelangelo to survive. It is known that he usually did not bother to make a preparatory model before beginning a sculp-ture. It was given by Cosimo I to Ammannati, one of Miche-langelo's closest followers, who in turn presented it to the Ac-cademia delle Arti del Disegno in 1583. This was the first of all art academies founded in 1563 by Vasari, Ammannati and oth-er leading artists of the time, who elected Michelangelo, to-gether with Cosimo I, as the first Academicians.

The torso was 'rediscovered' by the sculptor Adolf Hilde-brand (1847-1921) in 1906, who had been living in Florence since 1874 at the ex convent of San Francesco di Paola.

Bozzetti, attributed to Michelangelo and his circle

In 2000 a room in Casa Buonarroti was beautifully arranged with ten *bozzetti*, or small models in wax, terracotta and gesso attributed to Michelangelo and his circle. In the centre the terracotta of *Two Wrestlers* is now generally accepted as being by Michelangelo's own hand and dated around 1530. Although the other models were mostly only rediscovered in the 19th century and their provenance is often unknown, some of them are also now considered to be works by Michelangelo, including the tiny wood *Crucifix* (probably a late work of around 1562) and the early wax *River God* (about 1525).

Also displayed here with attributions to Michelangelo are a terracotta *Female Nude* and a *Male Torso*. There are also three copies from works by Michelangelo, one a terracotta *Madonna and Child* attributed to Vincenzo Danti, another a *Male Nude* in wax, and the third a gesso relief of the *Deposition* made after 1579. The last two works are by 16th century Florentine followers of Michelangelo.

Two Wrestlers

SANTO SPIRITO

Crucifix

It is known that Michelangelo carved a *Crucifix* for the prior of Santo Spirito, in return for being allowed by him to study anatomy in the Augustinian convent by dissecting the corpses of the dead. This *Crucifix* had been put on the high altar of the church. A *Crucifix* made of painted poplar wood, which had been heavily repainted, was found in the convent in 1963 and most scholars believe this is Michelangelo's *Crucifix* (although others have attributed it to Taddeo Curradi). It had been removed in the 17th century when the Baroque high altar was installed and was thought to have been lost at that time. It shows the slight figure of Christ in an unusual *contrapposto* serpentine position, a design later frequently copied. It is thought that this representation of Christ could have beeen influenced by Savonarola, who spoke of "*Cristo fragile*". The Cross itself is not original, and was probably added in the late 18th or early 19th century, although the *titulus Crucis* in Hebrew, Greek and Latin is original. After its discovery it was kept in the Casa Buonarroti, but in 2000 was removed for restoration and then returned to Santo Spirito where it is now displayed in the sacristy.

SANTA CROCE

Giorgio Vasari
Michelangelo's tomb

This monument was designed by Giorgio Vasari, who was a friend and collaborator of Michelangelo, and who wrote his biography in his famous *Vite*. The bust is by Battista Lorenzi, who also sculpted the allegorical figure of *Painting* which is flanked by *Sculpture* by Valerio Cioli and *Architecture* by Giovanni dell'Opera. The fresco of the *Pietà* is by Giovanni Battista Naldini. When Michelangelo thought to be buried in Rome he had intended his sculpture of the *Pietà* (now in the Museo dell'Opera del Duomo) to mark his tomb, but he later decided to request that his body be brought to Florence after his death. Apparently some of his contemporaries, including Daniele da Volterra, suggested his statue of *Victory* should be used as his funerary monument, but Vasari objected that he had never been a 'soldier' in his life ("he was never a soldier who conquered anyone, although he did conquer art by his virtue..."), and he felt his *Pietà* would have been far more suitable. But in the end it was decided to use neither and erect this rather disappointing memorial to him instead. His elaborate funeral service was held in San Lorenzo, but it was logical that he be buried here since Santa Croce had become the place where the most notable citizens of Florence were recorded and was to remain so for many centuries (Ghiberti, Machiavelli, Dante, and Galileo all have monuments here).

It is fitting that Michelangelo lies close to the monument which records Dante, who died in exile in 1321 and was buried in Ravenna, since the sculptor was a great admirer of his (and Dante was the subject of two of his sonnets) and we know that at one time Michelangelo had wished to design a fitting monument to him (Dante was only provided with one in 1829 when the present neoclassical work was erected by Stefano Ricci).

PONTE SANTA TRINITA

Although this was commissioned by Cosimo I from Bartolomeo Ammannati and begun in 1567, three years after Michelangelo's death, it is probable that Ammannati submitted his design to Michelangelo for his approval.

It is the most beautiful bridge across the Arno, and the flat arches, perfectly proportioned, known as catenaries (from *catena*, chain) which span the river recreate the unique curve of a chain suspended from two terminal points. The present bridge is an exact replica of the original blown up in 1944. It was built by Riccardo Gizdulich and Emilio Brizzi in 1955-57 and financed by public subscription from a committee presided over by Bernard Berenson.

Stefano Ricci,
Monument to Dante